THE TRUTH OF CREATION

The Truth of Creation

... and a Personal Testimony

Norman Lloyd

W.N. LLOYD
Barnsley

Published by W.N. Lloyd
<normanlloyd@hotmail.co.uk>

ISBN-13: 978 0 9554256 0 8
ISBN-10:   0 9554256 0 3

Printed in Great Britain.

Contents

Preface

I am just a man, in this world for a time, appointed, saved by grace at the age of forty three years old, now sixty years old and called to write the words of God.

This book is written and inspired by God to reach his people of all ages, the whosoever throughout the world, so that they might know, see and understand God in a new and glorious light. It is written with the hope that all may want to know Him, giving them a reason, purpose and destiny for their lives. I write from revelation in a moment in time, I am an instrument of God to reveal His words to help the people of this world before I depart.

The key is 'understanding' the word of God, because there is a lot of misunderstanding of his word. If you don't know or understand God's plan from the beginning of creation itself nothing makes sense. Understanding alone doesn't mean you will make the right decision in life. You see in the beginning was the end also, God sealed it there and then, and his word cannot be changed. All the events in the Bible will come to pass, some have come to pass already. You need to know the reason of God's purpose for your life at this time in creation, the reason you or I live. I know these words I write are from my Lord or I would not have written them. I write them from the kingdom for the kingdom. Any rewards these words may acquire, will stay in the kingdom for the kingdom. I know these words will cause debate throughout the world; the proud will stand against the truth of these words. The Lord knows of these people who will be exposed by their

9

opposition to these words of truth. I pray for people of the world not to understand me or see me in these words, but God the writer, they must see and understand. Some people, after a lifetime of teaching God's word in good heart will shake their heads in disbelief of these words saying within themselves, 'these words are wrong', while deep within their hearts knowing they are true. God wants these people to stand firm and humble themselves and accept the truth and revelation of these words. From these words the whole conception of how you interpret and teach God's word from the Bible will change, every misunderstanding of God's word in the Bible will become crystal clear. I pray that every lock will be opened in your hearts of understanding of our mighty God with his words of the truth of creation.

You may ask yourselves who is this man who writes these things, God shows me that I am like unto another man in scripture.

> There was a little city and few men within it; and there came a great king against it, and besieged it, and built great bulwarks against it. Now there was found in it a poor wise man, and he by his wisdom delivered the city; yet no man remembered that same poor man. Then said I wisdom is better than strength: never the less the poor man's wisdom is despised, and the words are not heard. The words of wise men are heard in quiet more than the cry of him that rule among fools. Wisdom is better than weapons of war: but one sinner destroyed much good. (Eccles 9: 14–18)

My words are not taxing but of a simple truth, not displaying my intelligence or intellectuality, with some help and technical information from the world's structures and of our humanity. There may be a certain amount of repetition which has been unavoidable.

THE TRUTH OF CREATION

The beginning

I attended a meeting one Sunday morning as usual, in April 2005. God spoke to me, in that meeting clearly, saying that I had to write a book. At the same time He gave me the title, *The Truth Of Creation*.

Immediately after the meeting I told my pastor what God had said. Straight away he took me on one side and prayed for me for God's guidance and he encouraged me to be obedient to the word of God. When I met up with him later and told him that I had started writing, he said, 'If everybody was that obedient to God, this world would be a different place'. Later my pastor came to see me at my home and read my preface. We had a good time as we spoke of the Lord and I believe that the Holy Spirit confirmed to us both that it is a God-inspired book. Before he left he encouraged me to get writing.

It's a miracle that God has called me to write anything at all, because I am not a good writer. At school I was always making mistakes, the teachers said that I thought too fast for my pen; so that I was always missing out letters. Sometimes I even spell my name wrong. In the early days I used to write and then ask my wife to read it, because I couldn't read my own writing. On the other hand I can easily work out anything mathematical. I believe God sums me up in Scripture in,

But God hath chosen the foolish things of the world to confound the wise; and God has chosen the weak things of the world to confound the things which are mighty. (1 Cor 1:27)

I have had to buy a new computer and printer, which I have never used, nor had any experience of before, so it's a slow process, but praise the Lord for the spell check. The reason I have pointed out all this personal information is that God must have a good sense of humour, to call me to write anything, so He has got to be in it, or I simply couldn't do it.

> In Matthew, 7:7–8 Jesus says, 'Ask, and it shall be given you; seek, and ye shall find; knock, and it shall be opened unto you. For everyone that asketh receiveth; and he that seeketh findeth; and to him that knocketh it shall be opened'.

I encourage you to adhere to these precious words of Jesus himself, written above. These words are prominent in my life, because it is a fact most people, never stop seeking. Our indwelling desire is to know more and more. It is such an exciting life, particularly as a Christian, seeing the truth of creation revealed, why you and I exists. This life cannot be comprehended by itself without God, because without Him nothing exists. When you are aware of Him you can see life and participate in it. So at this moment in time I am participating in God's plan by writing of Him my creator. By the will of God I write these things. If you plan a job, you cannot plan it if you don't plan it finished. For example If Michel angelo sculptured anything he must have envisaged the finish before he started or he would not know where to start. You cannot leave it to chance, or you will fail. In the beginning, God, before anything existed. He was, from this position our mighty God and, as in the Michel angelo example, had to see within Himself creation finished before He started to create anything, seen or unseen. Everything had to be sealed and perfect within Him – the beginning and the end – before He even started to create heaven and earth or anything that is. He never left anything to chance. No man knows fully, the mind of God; his depth is completely unreachable. But He has revealed Himself through his people, prophets, apostles, the Holy Spirit, Satan and Jesus the son of God, who was with God in the beginning of creation. There would be no point in creation, without the revelation of a loving God, a creator who created all things unto Himself.

> And God saw everything that He made, and behold it was very good. (Gen 1:31)

> He hath made everything beautiful in his time: also he hath set the world in their heart, so that no man can find out the work that God maketh from the beginning to the end. (Ecclesiastes 3–11)

God didn't make anything without reason or purpose – not one thing. Some things I write will seem obvious to you; but things only become obvious when revealed and understood.

In *our* worldly wisdom we would probably make a world full of good only, with no evil, conflict or sin. Many people ask, why God created this world; we cannot make sense of it – the struggle, the evil the fear of our fellow men, some of whom are consumed with hate, unforgiveness, murder, lust, greed, jealousy, the worldly battle of selfishness. You may ask yourself what the point is in all this battle; we are going to die anyway. And so we say to ourselves: Let's go and take what we can, let us have the best . . . by what ever means . . . as quickly as possible.

However let's now imagine we are in a position of God our creator who made all things from a position of nothingness, He is obviously not going to create anything that He hasn't got complete control over – even the devil – righteous will always prevail.

> Through faith we understand that the worlds were framed by the word of God, so that things which are seen were not made of things which do appear. (Heb 11:3)

Try to imagine how you would create this world and universe. Would you make it differently? Remember you are thinking from a position of knowledge, experience and something. You are also in a position of judgment, because you are something and not in nothingness – void of anything or life. Yes, I agree it's hard to get your head round the position of nothing. Where would we start? If all mankind clubbed together with all their knowledge and understanding and from our position of experience we would still get it wrong. For instance scientists don't even know why we die, why cells change from healing and growing, to degeneration and death. So let's go to a position of one who doesn't believe in God. From this position people are told there must have been a big bang. So there must have existed something of substance to bang. What caused it to bang? And, where did the substance come from? Some also say that we came from the sea as some sort of fish and evolved into man. Where did the sea and the fish come from? Some say that we evolved from monkeys. So why aren't we still evolving into something else? And why didn't all the monkeys evolve? Why were some left behind? Has someone pressed a button and stopped evolution? Or is there a selection process of who evolves and who doesn't? Yes there are many unanswered questions, God says we will never know all things. Anyway let's go again and ask ourselves what we would change in creation. Most people would not have evil in this world, but it is feasible that others don't like goody goodies, so they could support a position of evil. I have given only these two opposite examples of good and evil to make my point, so I ask you (bearing in mind you're thinking as a non-believer) only to believe what you see, or in the big bang. How could you create good and evil from any substance or matter? It's impossible. Yet we know they exist. They can only be seen if demonstrated from and in a state of morality and judgment. How could we create either of them from nothing? There is no explanation other than that the answer exists with God Himself. You see, faith is believing something unseen, you believe it exists, but you cannot see it, so in this example, we all have a measure of faith. From a position of believing good and evil exist, plus other examples of jealousy, greed, guilt, hate, envy, lust, love, etc. Again you cannot see them; but through faith you know they exist. You only see them when they are exercised intern-ally and externally, affecting your very life. So from the truth that these concepts exist – not from or in a solid state seen, but unseen in spirit – why not believe in a creator God who also exists in spirit unseen. Reader please study carefully what I have just written, don't just brush these facts aside, you don't have to have faith that these concepts exist. You know they do, just like the air you breath which you can't see but you know it's there. Ask yourself the question; you deserve an answer. Where did these unseen concepts come from? Only by faith can you believe.

I have written from many points of life trying to awaken in the reader a deeper enthusiasm for God our creator. The most important and repeated word is 'opposite'. We all obviously know that there are probably hundreds; simple ones like plus and minus, beginning and end. One cannot exist without the other, it's impossible. God knew that we needed opposites before anything was. Without an opposite one cannot exist or, have meaning or value, or measure. God made all things, including opposites, revealed in His creation, because again there would be no meaning, value, or recognition and measure of His love without the opposite hate. God knew before any-thing was that it is impossible for man to comprehend love without an opposite, it cannot exist. We would just be like gold-fish in a bowl. You could not even say the word, or know God as a loving creator. The question is how did He introduce oppos-ites on earth and in mankind from the beginning, so that we too could have the same as God and be in His image? The book of Revelation tells us about the war in heaven,

> Michael and his angels fought against the dragon; and the dragon fought and his angels. And prevailed not; neither was there place found anymore in heaven. And the great dragon was cast out, that old serpent, called the devil, and Satan, which deceiveth the whole world: he was cast out into the earth, and his angels were cast out with him. (Chapter 12: 7–9)

So, as scripture shows God in his wisdom made opposite angels, good and bad, because again you cannot have one without the other, both sides used as instruments for God, of God, from God, for chastisement, righteousness and recognition on earth.

> The Lord has made all things for Himself yea, even the wicked for the day of evil. (Proverbs 16:4)

So Lucifer, the angel who become the devil was made by God to be beautiful and proud. But he wanted God's position; which led to a fight and the casting to earth of the tempter. The devil was the first sinner against God, made to lose the fight, because sin cannot prevail in heaven. God cast him to earth, to be used by God in His perfect plan for revelation, recognition and temptation which exposes and chastisement, because sin can't be chastised without it being revealed or recognized, without the opposite in creation on earth. The devil's character is written in scripture:

> How art thou fallen from heaven, O Lucifer, son of the morning. (Isaiah 14:12)

> Thou were perfect in thy ways from the day that thou was created. (Ezekiel 28:15)

and again where sinful thoughts entered Lucifer's mind,

> Thine heart was lifted up because of thy beauty; thou has corrupted thy wisdom by reason of thy brightness. (Ezekiel 28:17)

It's maybe hard at this point for the reader to grasp and understand the mind of God, in that He actually and purposely created Lucifer (the liar), because life could not be life without him, with no opposite to Jesus (the truth), who sits on the right, or righteous side of God. Once again you can't have a right side without a left side, It is emphasized numerous times that Jesus sits on the right.

> Hereafter shall the son of man sit on the right hand of the power of God?. (Luke 22:69)

> Who is gone into heaven, and is on the right hand of God; angels and authorities and powers being made subject to him. (Peter 3:22)

> So then after the Lord had spoken unto them, he was received up into heaven, and sat on the right hand of God. (Mark 16:19)

Why not say that Jesus just sits with God? Because there have got to be two sides to God, or it's no point or of any other reason to even mention the righteous side.

> A wise man's heart is at his right hand, but a fool's heart at his left. (Ecclesiastes 10:2)

> Then shall he say also unto them on the left hand, depart from me, ye cursed, into everlasting fire, prepare for the devil and his angels. (Mathew 25:41)

These scriptures shows the value God puts on using the words right and left.

> Mine hand also hath laid the foundation of the earth, and my right hand hath spanned the heavens. (Isaiah 48:13)

So here we have the devil on earth in God's plan to lie and tempt Eve to eat of the forbidden fruit. At least Eve argued with the devil not to take of the fruit, Adam just took it from Eve and ate it with no argument, they both took it together, carrying out God's plan, disobeying Him.

> And the Lord God said, the man is become as one of us, to know good and evil. And now, lest he put forth his hand, and take also of the tree of life, and eat, and live forever. . . . (Genesis 3:22)

So without the devil on earth to tempt and lie to Eve she would never have taken & eaten the fruit of the tree; it's impossible. So God's perfect plan for man to have knowledge of good and evil (opposites) came to pass as God had planned. Sin entered the world from God, because the fruit was from both sides of God and so man being in His image, as in scripture above, man has become one of us, like God.

So God's plan for man to have the knowledge of good and evil came to pass, I must emphasize at this point that it was knowledge, of good and evil, as we have today, but as then and now, we don't have to do either, we have our free will to choose. You see you cannot be tempted by the devil to sin in anything that you have no knowledge of. So if God hadn't told Adam and Eve of the tree of good and evil they could not be tempted of it, or receive of it. Some people argue about man's fall, as though man got it wrong disobeying God; but I tell you it was perfectly planned by God, who at this point didn't give Eve the attributes to resist the devil. He could have done, but He didn't, because it just had to be, to be in His image. Would you think God being God would risk His plan to fail, putting the destiny of all creation in the hands of Adam and Eve, and the devil? No, He put the tree of good and evil there purposely, so that good and evil, the opposites, would enter into mankind and this world. He didn't have to put the tree there.

Ask yourselves, why was it there? God can do all things, He didn't have to put it there. So Adam and Eve took of both sides of God, good and evil, left and right, righteousness and unrighteousness, oppos-ites, so then we would be in His image as He had planned.

> And God said, 'Let us make man in our image, after our like-ness . . .'. (Genesis 1:26)

The tree could not stand or be recognised without opposite values, good and evil, it's impossible to take one without the other, because they cannot exist, with any value, measure, or recognition, thereof. You must see this truth from a new cre-ative view point and not from your worldly position now, having already received both within yourself, the knowledge of good and evil. Knowing this, and from your present posi-tion, you would probably only want to make good. But if only good was made in creation, without its opposite, you would not know what good was.

> So He drove out the man; and He placed at the east of the garden of Eden cherubims, and a flaming sword which turned every way, to keep the way of the tree of life. (Genesis 3:24)

> The thief cometh not, but for to steal, and to kill, and to destroy; I am come that they might have life, and that they might have it more abundantly, Jesus said. (John 10:10)

The same tree of life that was spoken of in Eden, that was man-ifest as man for you and me, to set an example that we might follow, planned by God in creation, that man is Jesus Christ our saviour, the righteous opposite planned from the beginning.

> Who hath saved us, and called us with an holy calling, not accord-ing to our works, but according to His own purpose and grace,

which was given us in Jesus Christ before the world began, but is now made mani-fest by the appearing of our saviour Jesus Christ, who hath abolished death, and hath brought life and immortality to light though the gospel. (2 Tim, 1:9–10)

Because the devil beguiled and lied to Eve, God said,

And I will put enmity between thee and the woman, and between thy seed and her seed; it shall bruise thy head, and thou shall bruise his heel. (Gen 3:15)

This scripture speaks into the future of Christ's birth, sufferings and sacrifice and Satan's ultimate defeat, demonstrated on the cross. So God drove out man from Eden because of his sin, separating him from the love of God through the tree of life, which is the way to heaven, Jesus, the sword, guarded by the Holy Spirit, never will and never could sin entered heaven. So the scene is set, sin separates, not only from God, but from each other, as it does today. So the question is how did God plan to redeem us back to Himself and Eden after the fall. Remember you cannot be redeemed back to a position that you hadn't come from, or fallen from in the first place; Likewise there is no point in redemption or its existence if there was no reward, because there would be no desire for you to return. But God had a desire for you to return from the beginning. You cannot have a new covenant without an old one, or a new law without an old law. If we didn't need a new covenant Jesus Christ, who was the new covenant, planned from the beginning, would be of no effect.

Hebrews. 8:7, written by Paul, says 'For if that first covenant had been faultless then no place have been sought for the second'.

God knew before creation that we needed an old covenant so that Jesus, planned from the beginning, could be the new covenant, so that we can recognise the old from the new, giving us value and measure of the sacrifice Jesus made for you and me. Again new without old cannot exist. What a God! We would have got it all wrong. So Jesus died on the cross sinless. He willingly, sacrificed Himself for our sins and He rose again, conquering over, self, sin and death, again planned by God from the beginning. Alleluia. God didn't say oops, I got that wrong. Er, what do I do about sin? Oh I know I'll send Jesus as an example to die on the cross, because I got it wrong, that is the only alternative to these words I write, so I've answered it before you ask it, to save your embarrassment, God made nothing in vain. What a plan. Do you realise, love and forgiveness were demonstrated on the cross? you couldn't demonstrate forgiveness without having something to forgive, and that is why sin had to enter the world. Again, I repeat, from the beginning of creation, God planned sin to come in the world, or we wouldn't have recognition, or know the difference, because there wouldn't be a difference. Jesus would have died for nothing. But God says all have sinned and need to be saved. Without it redemption from sin would have no value. Only through Jesus Christ can you be saved from sin and self and be redeemed to where you came from in eternity, with our father God, and Jesus.

Jesus saith unto him, I am the way, the truth, and the life: no man cometh unto the father, but by me. (John 14:6)

For God so loved the world, that He gave His only begotten Son, that whosoever believeth in Him should not perish, but have everlasting life. (John 3:16)

I am speaking to you about the kingdom of God, which is not of this world's system; only through Jesus can you know the difference. If you don't know Jesus you will never know of the kingdom, or of the existence of a choice.

I love them that love me; and those that seek me early shall find me. (Proverbs 8:17)

For even hereunto were ye called: because Christ also suffered for us, leaving us an example, that ye should follow His steps. (Peter 2:21)

Again Peter, who was with Jesus personally on this earth, speaks of Jesus' sacrifice, without which, you wouldn't have a choice.

Who his own self bore our sins in his own body on the tree that we, being dead to sin, should live unto righteousness: by whose stripes ye were healed. (Peter 2:24)

He that covereth his sins shall not prosper: but whoso confesseth and forsaketh them shall have mercy. (Proverbs 28:13)

The devil was defeated in the beginning, but to defeat him in our personal lives, we must follow the example that Jesus set before us, by sacrificing our lives to sin and self too. Everything was not, but now is, and one day it will not be, even you, who are temporary. So as scripture says, make your choice soon; yes, you do have a choice, without the opposite you wouldn't have a choice, so I encourage you to make the right choice, and give your life to Jesus. You know it makes sense. You can't make sense of this silly world, where dog eats dog. God needs you also in his kingdom, to represent Him, to show His truth love and glory for mankind and to draw us back from sin and despair, to a future with God, our father and maker and to everlasting life. We need to be conformed to Jesus Christ, who is the end of all knowledge. Your thoughts, or any thoughts can never be original, because nothing is new under the sun to God our maker, but you can have a new life revealed through His son Jesus. He doesn't want you to share your life with him, He wants it totally. From the beginning the battle was won, but the world's spiritual war for our souls carries on, God is still walking about on earth as He did in Eden by His Holy Spirit, wanting to speak with you through His Son Jesus. Stop fighting and be set free from the rudiments of this world. Don't worship creation, but the Creator. Start again. If you are not satisfied with your old life, have a new one, go back to Eden, heaven on earth, don't waste that sacrifice Jesus made on your selfish self.

In the Truth of Creation, I personally couldn't even write to you without man taking from the tree of good and evil that God put in the Garden of Eden, (opposites), it's like unto a baby who when born takes it's first breath of God and becomes alive, man also came alive in God and in His image when he took of the tree in Eden, which without there would be nothing to debate of any subject, because there wouldn't be a subject, or have a difference of opinion about anything, you couldn't even have an opinion. The battle of good and evil on the television or news couldn't exist, no dreams, no news, no difference, nothing to talk about, no cinema, no books, no battles, no wars, no hope, no desires, no future, no good, no evil, no redemption, no born again, no lies, no truth. I'll leave you the reader to imagine other states that you cannot have without opposites, but wait a minute you can't have an imagination, or think of these things without an opposite. We would not need our minds to work things out or decide right from wrong, I couldn't even write this book, it couldn't exist. We would be like a tree for example, it grows bigger and dies like us, but the other thing it does it reproducers, without thought or reward, or joy or love in its offspring, no spirit, or choice, unlike us. We would be similar to the tree also without the opposite, and made in Gods image, to be able to receive good and evil and all Gods fruits and to minister these fruits as we choose through our free will, (no opposite, no choice).

From this place in Gods plan without the opposite, you could never know God as love, demonstrated and planned through the sacrifice of His only begotten son Jesus Christ, WOW! That's the only hope we have, to know God through Jesus and be redeemed back to Him because He loves us so much. Hope again cannot exist without the opposite, because you can only hope for something different or better, or go from sin, to a sinless state giving it value and measure. You cannot continue to progress without the opposite, progress to where, without the opposite there isn't a where, or to, or loss, or gain, or reward, or progression. There would be no point Jesus coming and representing righteousness, planned from the beginning, but because God new that sin, unrighteousness, the opposite planned by Him would be in the world. There would be no value in the sacrifice Jesus made if it was in vain, Jesus came to take away the sin of the world, because of love. Without the moving of positions there can be no value or recognition, or the desire to move if it isn't a better position, positions cannot exist without opposites. The better position is to move to a sinless state, without sin to start with, movement is impossible and impossible to have a better state, because there is no state, without Jesus victory over sin, what a God who new all this in the beginning of creation, that sin had to enter the world or there is no movement at all, because it's impossible to have movement without the opposite to sin which is Jesus, the redeemer, planned from the beginning. So the devil was made by God perfectly and not in vain to do Gods perfect plan and will, even to this day, so could we say, in certain circumstances, thank God for the devil, the chastising tool of God and exposure of our sin, the opposite to Jesus, even giving Jesus a reason to come planned by God in the beginning or there would be no point in Him coming or His sacrificial victory, no devil or sin, no victory, no battle, no reason to strive, no hope, no point, no relationship, no difference, no love, what a God, without the tree of good and evil, and the devil, the opposite, there would be nothing to write about, there would not even be a Bible.

The Truth About Life in General

You are not here really, because you are temporary – your mortal body that is. Anything temporary doesn't exist in eternity. So it's not you that we see, because you are on the inside of your mortal frame. You can waste your money all your life pampering the outside, but it won't change you or anything from being mortal, or change you on the inside. So when mortality comes, your spirit that has been in control of your body will need a new home. Your spirit never dies. So you have two choices, heaven or hell. The question is did you at any point give your life to Jesus, bringing life to your living death, so that He could change and purify your inside, in preparation for an eternal life with Him in heaven? If you haven't done this yet, please choose wisely before it's too late. The alternative, well I'll be blunt, it's hell.

Are you a when person? one who says life will be all right when I pass my exams; when I get a job; when I have plenty of money; when I get married; when I get a house; when I have a swimming pool; when I have a snooker table; when I have a flat-screen television; when I get that car; when I've paid my mortgage off; when I've children; when I have grand-children. We've all got our own desires of 'whens', I tell you they are all an illusion a lie within one's mind. When, 'when' comes you are still not satisfied so you go on to the next 'when'. I'm sorry but your hope was in vain, because your next 'when' will let you down, no 'when' of this world can ever satisfy you're in-built yearning for complete satisfaction of the soul; only Jesus can. So are you young looking forward? Well don't listen to the people who say it will be all right 'when'. Or are you an older person? Look back, then; look back at your life at all the 'whens', think for a while and honestly answer for yourself, was it all right 'when'? Are you working hard to receive the next 'when', saying to yourself when I get to this 'when', everything will be all right. How many 'whens' do you want? When are you going to learn? The devil is wafting you on in life, getting you to live the lie. I tell you, you are being duped. You are wasting your life on the 'whens' of this world.

Only an indwelling Christ can satisfy your soul and life. 'When' is when you are going to heaven after your short stay on earth. It doesn't matter when you go, it's where you are going that counts. It's the only 'when' I earnestly desire, because it's eternal. The worldly 'whens' are peripheral and temporary. So are you going to listen to the robber with a life of 'whens', where death is your reward; or unto Jesus and eternal life? Amen.

I see God and His communication like a mobile phone, it has no visible wires, but you can speak and see someone, even from the moon, or from space. Wow! So, mankind has now discovered that we can see, and have communication, through the air, this technology was here waiting to be discovered from the beginning of time. It is the same with God; but His communication is spiritual and His lines of communication have also been there from the beginning of time; but you can't see them. Everything was here from the beginning, it had to be, just waiting to be discovered by man. All the materials to build anything – even you – are from mother earth. The example that I've just written, I want you to be honest, If a hundred years ago and someone had told you of this technology, or even the existence of a computer that I'm using now, would you have believed them? I think you would say, no. Go further back to the life when folk believed that the earth was flat; or to when the wheel was invented: just think how that changed the world's transport system. Test the kids and see how many items they can list, that operate with a wheel. So man has come a long way down discovery alley. But that too will come to an end. It has to. There will, one day, be nothing else to discover. Jesus is coming back one day for His beloved, but he won't do so until everything is discovered that God put here in the beginning, or there would have been no point God putting them here in the first place. God made nothing in vain, so watch out when there is nothing new on the market, because Jesus is coming back, to gather His own unto Himself.

Can you imagine life with limited electricity and without natural resources, like gas, or oil? Because, there's no doubt about it, these things will run out one day. I predict chaos to come. The new term will be called localization, because there will be no fuel for transport, for things we need, so nothing will move very far, even us. What will we do without fuel and limited transport, with no planes, cars, trains, or machinery? It's going to happen folks. Get your teepees ready. I'll leave you to contemplate and debate this further amongst yourselves, because it's a massive subject just on it's own. All these changes are definitely going to take place; the point I'm trying to make is that God never changes. He is not interested in our affluence, He is only interested in whether we are living according to heavenly principles, demonstrated through His son, Jesus Christ. Man keeps changing the morality barriers . . . in the work place, in schools and the like. When is it going to end? When are we going to get it perfect, with no more changes, so we know where we stand? I can tell you of a truth: man without God through Jesus Christ is, as scripture.

> Therefore whosoever heareth these sayings of mine, and doeth them, I will liken him unto a wise man, which built his house upon a rock. And the rain descended, and the floods came, and the winds

blew, and beat upon that house; and it fell not: for it was founded upon a rock. And everyone that heareth these sayings of mine, and doeth them not, shall be likened unto a foolish man, which built his house upon the sand. And the rain descended, and the floods came, and the winds blew, and beat upon that house; and it fell: and great was the fall of it. And it came to pass, when Jesus had ended these sayings, the people were astonished at His doctrine. (Mt. chapter 7: 24–28)

So the parable is giving you an example. It asks if your life is built on a good foundation, one of God's word of righteousness and truth that never needs to change – because it is the truth and there is only one truth, which sets you free. So, whatever life throws at you, you will be able to stand firm and deal with it. Alternatively, if your life is built on shaky ground of lies, a go-along-with-life without God you are vulnerable to this world's system of change and selfishness. You will never know the peace, purpose and joy that God intended for you. Let me try and give you an example of your being, the inner workings of your body function without thought, everything is in auto mode. Clearly you can operate some things in manual, such as breathing, but you can't control the inner parts, such as your heart. So what about the the spiritual side of us? I see strings of communication going direct to God, as though they are hanging down from God and our free will to choose the good ones or the bad ones. You are like a puppet on strings of communication from God. It's who you are and how you behave, it's your choice. So who is pulling your strings – the good ones, Jesus, or the bad ones, represented by the devil? One leads to heaven and one leads to hell. I encourage you to latch onto the truth and love of Jesus. It will change your lines of communication, direct to heaven, leading to peace on earth and goodwill to all men. If you latch yourself to the wrong lines, you will have no peace and hell on earth as your destiny. God made all spirits. They are His to do His command at His will, So all spirits, good or evil, are obedient to Him. So as a spiritual being, made by God from the beginning, He knows your spiritual content at any time. That means He owns you too. You are not your own.

> The earth is the Lord's, and the fullness thereof; the world, and they that dwell therein. (Psalm 24:1)

> If I ascend into heaven, thou art there: if I make my bed in hell, behold, thou art there . . . Yea, the darkness hideth not from thee; but the night shineth as the day: the darkness and the light are both alike to thee. (Psalm 139:8, 12)

> The eyes of the Lord are in every place, beholding the evil and the good. (Proverbs 15:3)

> For nothing is secret, that shall not be made manifest; neither anything hid, that shall not be known and come abroad. (Luke 8:17)

Everyone will have to give account of themselves one day to Jesus, whether you believe in God or not. So choose wisely before its too late. Latch on to the right communication to God, on a direct line though Jesus Christ our Lord, and be saved.

An example of Opposites

I would like you to contemplate on the things of this world, that we take for granted, but are perfect and which we can't live without. It's the obvious example of opposites, carbon dioxide and oxygen, which is unseen, man eventually discovered these true facts of existence, and that one cannot exist without the other. We obviously breathe in oxygen and breathe out carbon dioxide and vegetation does the opposite. Wow! Could a big bang have created this? Can you try to get your head round this simple truth – though not simple from a creative view point – that we take for granted. If you were the creator, would you have thought of just this one thing that had to be, for anything to exist at all? In this example it proves my point that everything had to be sealed and perfect in creation before man came. Before it was, God obviously had to know our needs of oxygen and importantly get the balance right, before we were created, or creation wouldn't work. Can you try to contemplate, that everything breathes, automatically, without thought, or programming, even when sleeping. I don't know about you, but I think it's an amazing reality, looking from a creative and a new beginning of God's perfect plan. What a God!

Light and Darkness

In the first chapter of Genesis, God said, Let there be light. You see again you cannot in a new creation have any measure of light, or know, or describe light without darkness. There would be no comprehension of either darkness or light, one without the other cannot be, or be described, or any name given to that state. So, in Genesis 5, the outcome of darkness and light, was one day, which gave us measure of time and age, plus God knew we would have to sleep as part of that one day to recover for the next day – which again we take for granted. Reader, do you realise what had to be in existence to produce light and darkness? Let me explain a simple truth that we know and accept today. Isaac Newton, a godly man wrote. 'The exquisite structure of the sun, the planets and the comets, could not have had their origin, but by a plan and absolute dominion of an intelligent and powerful being'. The sun's intensity; its spectrum of different light, distance, and movement; obviously without these we would never exist. God knew about all this before anything was.

> For the invisible things of him from the creation of the world are clearly seen, being understood by the things that are made, even his eternal power and Godhead; so that they are without excuses. (Romans 1:20)

> He stretcheth out the north over the empty place, and hangeth the earth upon nothing. (Job 26:7)

We understand from history that once-upon-a-time people believed the world was flat and that we might fall off the end. But mankind discovered the reality, that it was round. Also, in 1475, by thanks to a man called Copernicus we discovered the truth that the earth is in space part of a system of planets instead of at the centre of the universe. Let's take the earth itself. It revolves at 1037 miles per hour and hurtles round the sun at 67,000 mph. It's tilted at 23.5 degrees in reference to the sun to give us our seasons. It stays in the same relative place in the solar system, although it is moving yet there's 94.5 million miles between the earth and the sun. It's another 'Wow'!. Can you see, reader of *The Truth of Creation*, all these statistics had to be precise for any form of life to exist. I will give you some more stats to prove my point. Venus is very like the earth, except its surface temperature is 470 degrees centigrade, because the sun's rays reach it two minutes before us. At the other extreme is Mars, which is a little further away from the sun than us and is a frozen waste. Another incredible fact is the moon's gravitational influence, which gives us the tides and also keeps the earth steady for a long and successful development of life; without the moon's influence the earth would wobble like a dying top. Then we have our atmosphere – like a blanket over us – without which our temperature would be minus 50 degrees centigrade. I'm not writing a book on the planets, but as I stated earlier about light and dark, it had to be written, because everything is relative to each other for life to exist. Einstein's theory of relativity fascinates me. In God's creation it is a fact that all life relies on something else to sustain it. The world moves at the exact speed with its constant mass and distance from the sun which determines perfect gravitational pull, and a sustained position to keep us on the earth. In His wisdom God knew this and gave us a muscular body to move around, which makes us tired, so we need sleep and recovery, all in one day: like opposites, light and dark.

The earth

Now let's put our feet on the earth, everything in our eco system relies on something else. Everything needs sustenance, to exist in the first place, to sustain existence and everything has to reproduce, or nothing could exist, or live without someone, or something else to rely on. Can you try to imagine God in His mind? He had to have everything in its place before He even started to create anything, such as reproduction of food and automatic reproduction capabilities for every living thing, man, birds, fish, animals, insects, grass, trees and all vegetation, even the worm He considered. I'm not going deeper into this subject, but it would be a good exercise, just what you yourself need, or rely on, to sustain you or animals, on earth. Just think of the kangaroo. When it is born, instinctively it crawls the right way into the pouch. Why does it have a pouch? Because, as we all know, the mother jumps and the baby would fall to the ground otherwise. See if you can think of more of life's miracles that we take for granted.

I know it's a massive subject, but it's fascinating to think about how big God is, providing such infinite detail to life on earth. So if someone tells me it just happened by chance, my reply would be, Get a life.

All things were created by Him and for Him. And He is before all things and by Him all things consist. (Col 1:16–17)

Wet, Dry, Fire and Salt

Another opposite is wet and dry. 'God called the dry land earth and the waters seas'. Gen 1:10. It's obvious again, but land cannot be called dry, if it isn't totally void of water. Again God knew from the beginning that we couldn't exist without water. Believers in the big bang, I ask you, How did water come to be only on earth and not on the other planets? Surely if it was evident before the bang, the bang would have caused it to disperse onto other planets in our galaxy. Or, how did water exist in the first place? Why was it here? It's not alive, but every living thing needs it to live. The unbeliever cannot explain it, and only by faith can anyone believe, that God created all things – even water. He knew before anything was, that without this strange liquid nothing could live. Have you ever thought that water never gets any less although we and others drink it, it never leaves the earth (unless an astronaut had a little wee-wee on the moon, or in space). Water and fire as in the examples of Sodom and Gomorrah and the Ark, cannot kill evil spirits, you can only kill them in your life through Jesus Christ.

Think of the salt in the sea – evenly dispersed throughout the world, (apart from the Dead Sea). Have you thought that without the salt in the sea, the whole world would smell, with diseases galore. Without salt in our bodies man could not exist. I wonder how many millions of tons of salt there are in the sea. it doesn't really matter if we know the answer or not. But God our creator again knew from the beginning that we needed salt to exist and how much. Again, reader not one molecule of salt leaves the world, because if any was used up, as with water, the balance would change, the sea would get saltier, or less salty, so the balance stays perfect as God planned it Another 'wow!'.

Jealousy, Pride, Humility

Cain and Abel, were Adam's offspring. Cain killed Abel because of 'envy', or 'jealousy'. These words can be complex and very hard to explain, because they can have different meanings in different circumstances. Jealousy can mean to be discontent with your lot, or life, or self when your desire is to be like someone else, or to want what they have (belongings, house, car, wealth) or to strive artificially for acceptance of others. This can turn to hate, bitterness and spite and you want the worst to happen to them which can lead, as in Cain and Abel's case, to murder. Beware that you don't poke your head in the domain, or controlled area, of a jealous person. Although you have done nothing wrong to them and you are trying to help, a jealous person takes you to be a rival. So don't mix with them, or you could get hurt. A jealous person has a good memory for the wrong reason and is always looking for trouble in others. God says, Love yourself. It might seem a vain statement, but it means accept yourself as you are. There is practical reasoning in that you didn't choose to be born or choose your sex, colour, or creed. You didn't choose who your parents are, or their affluence, or how they brought you up. Take the royal family for example. They had no choice either. So don't knock them for their position. God looks at how you live your life, no matter what your circumstances are. The truth is He is no respecter of a person's, looks, position, colour, or affluence. God doesn't even see or recognise these worldly and temporary values that jealous people count important. It's the spiritual content in man, good or evil, that God sees and values, so I encourage you to accept yourself as you are. Live your life unto Jesus and not others. Eliminate jealousy, so that you can live a good and fruitful life, through Jesus Christ. You know it makes sense. Alleluia.

There is also divine jealousy

For I the *Lord* am a jealous God. (Ex. 20:5)

For thou shalt worship no other God: for the *Lord*, whose name is Jealous, is a jealous God. (Ex. 34:14)

This is God's own jealousy which is perfectly good, meaning to protect, and to be vigilantly watching over you, with a desire for you to do right, because He loves you so, he wants you redeemed back to Him, through Jesus Christ's example and sacrifice.

The opposite, pride, can have different meanings also if used in different contexts. For example, an 'I'm better than you' attitude, superiority, self-esteem; it's a complete 'self' thing – evil in fact. On the other hand you can take pride in a job well done, feeling gratified within yourself, a sense of achievement. These scriptures speak of pride,

For all that is in the world, the lust of the flesh, and the lust of the eyes, and the pride of life, is not of the Father, but is of the world. (1 John 2:16)

Pride goeth before destruction and a haughty spirit before a fall. (Peter 16:18)

When pride cometh, then cometh shame: but with the lowly is wisdom. (Peter 11:2)

There is much more scripture about pride, but the ultimate example of pride is the devil himself, who wanted something that he couldn't have, namely the pos-ition of God Himself.

Are you like that, do you want to be the top-dog in everything? If so, beware the frustration, because you will never
achieve it, because you cannot satisfy pride. It has no ending.
So pride is vanity, self-importance, conceit, self, snobbery, critical, etc. You can't see, or consider anyone but yourself, with
a mirror in every room, for self-adjustment and adoration.
Some husbands have never seen their wives without make-
up, because of pride and the fear of its opposite: shame and
rejection. I'm not being sexist in this example, because men
also wear make-up these days, if you look at the stash of cosmetics and the like that young men have, some are equal to
women. Everything has to be shaved nowadays; women have
got more shavers than men, some even trip down to the spray
booth to look like they have been on an expensive holiday.
You see brown is beautiful, but some of the community want
to be white. Tell me folks, do you agree, the world's gone mad
with no acceptance of who you are, we all have the same
colour blood. They ask, Do I look and smell nice? I say, No, it's
the make-up that looks nice and the perfume smells nice. But
that's not you. In fact I've never seen you in the natural. So
who are you?

Have you seen my car?

Yes, but who are you?

Have you seen my clothes and where I shop?

Yes, but who are you?

My children are at university you know.

Yes, but who are you?

Have you seen my house and garden? We have a cleaner and
a gardener you know.

Yes, but who are you?

Have you seen my jewelery.

Yes, but who are you?

We only go on expensive cruises and stay in the Hilton.

Yes, but who are you?

Yes I know you now. You live in the pride of life, on the external, not the internal, a proud person is deaf, and by the way do you know who you are? Well err, err, err. Err. Well I've got . . .

Yuk, *stop*! Nothing wrong folks with having things of this world, but if you live to them, you are dead already. You see, the fly on the wall, as they say, knows your secrets. He sees the bare essentials that you try to hide from everyone. I'll just let you ponder on that one for a moment . . . (No screaming please!) That 'fly' is Jesus Christ. You can't hide from Him, and He knows you better than you know yourself. Knowing you, He set the ultimate example, which is the opposite of pride, humility. He gave His life for you, yes you, and He nailed the worthless bit to the cross, the temporary body that proud people live to. Why not live to eternal things, which is Jesus himself? He wants to set the ultimate example of self-abasement, He wants to wash your feet; yes the son of God, even Jesus Christ, wants you to follow His example,

> He riseth from supper, and laid aside his garments; and took a towel, and girded himself. After that he poureth water into a basin, and began to wash the disciples' feet, and to wipe them with the towel wherewith he was girded. (John 13:4–5)
>
> For whosoever exalteth himself shall be abased; and he that humble himself shall be exalted. (Luke 14:11)
>
> Whosoever therefore shall humble himself as this little child, the same is the greatest in the kingdom of heaven. (Matthew 18:4)

You see you cannot teach a proud person anything, because they know it all already, but if you are as a child, humble, trusting, and easy to teach and eager to learn, you will grow in the grace of God, but pride will keep you ignorant of anything worthwhile, even God Himself. A current example is of a little girl, who calls me uncle and lives across the road from me. She is called Holly and has just won the British Championship 2005 at disco dancing, at five years old level. Her mum and dad have tried to tell her she's number one, but bless her, she says no I'm not I'm 198–her competition number. She never mentions it to anyone, or thinks anything about it; she has total humility, that's why Jesus says come to me as a little child, just like Holly Smith, full of joy; and loves others unconditionally. We can learn from children because they are not contaminated with the things of this world. I have given a few examples of envy, jealousy, pride and humility, again opposites, where one cannot exist without the other, but I must confess that you could write a book on this subject alone. Don't forget the ultimate example of humility was and is Jesus himself, He never boasted, but went to the cross, blameless, without a whimper of complaint and held His arms out saying,

Father, forgive them; for they know not what they do. (Luke, 23:34)

The ultimate servant of all.

Violence, Gentleness, Corruption, Honest

The earth also was corrupt before God, and the earth was filled with violence. (Gen 6:11)

This scripture was from Noah's time. The ark and the flood to eradicate violence and corruption in the people at that time. But, as you know, nothing has changed. These things are still with us today. Personally I see the ark as Jesus saying, come unto Me, come into the ark of My security and close the door on this violence and corruption, shut it out from your life, because only with Me will you have the oppos-ite, because I am the opposite which is in me of, (for violence), gentleness, meek-ness and mildness and (for corruption), honesty, ethicality, purity and morality. The example in Noah's time is the same today, you cannot eliminate sin from the world by physical death, because it's a spiritual life. You cannot kill a spirit by drowning; but you can eliminate sin from your life by giving your life to Jesus and dying to self. Come on folks, come into the ark where Jesus awaits you. Don't look back, and make sure you close the door of your old life fully. Don't leave the door ajar. It's all or nothing.

Come unto me, all ye that labour and are heavy laden, and I will give you rest. Take my yoke upon you, and learn of me; for I am meek and lowly in heart: and ye shall find rest unto your souls. For my yoke is easy, and my burden is light. (Mt. 11:28–30)

Blessing, Cursing

And I will bless them that bless thee, and curse him that curseth thee: and in thee shall all the families of the earth be blessed. (Gen 12:3)

Abraham was blessed with the promise of Christ in his genealogy; I also am blessed by giving my life to Jesus Christ and so coming into that same genealogy of Abraham and Christ.

Know ye therefore that they which are of faith, the same are the children of Abraham. (Gal 3:7)

So you can receive that same blessing only if you believe, which means divine protection, favour and support of God in this world, and the ultimate promise of heaven on earth and eternal life with our father God. God also mentions the opposite; cursing, which means trouble, condemnation and affliction, for which Christ took to the cross on our behalf. Again, in this example, protection can't exist without trouble; it would be meaningless, because you cannot be protected from nothing. So trouble, affliction and the curse of this world, can only be divinely protected from, through Jesus Christ and His sacrifice. Amen.

Love, Hate

Now Jacob loved Joseph more than all his children, because he was the son of his old age: and he made him a coat of many colors. And when his brethren saw that their father loved him more than all his brethren, they hated him, and could not speak peaceably unto him. (Gen 37:3–4)

This is the story of Joseph and his older brothers. It is written that his father loved Joseph more. It is similar to fathers today. It's not that you love your young children more, it's just they need you to give them more attention, and the older siblings are more reliant and make their own decisions. Joseph's brothers forgot that when they were young they in turn got the most attention and love. So jealousy took over, and they hated Joseph and even planned to kill him, although he had done nothing wrong to them. They sold him instead to passing travelers, and deceived their father into believing that he had been killed, creating such sorrow for him. This Bible story of love and hate is recurring today. The battle commences even in normal families, it's a spiritual battle of love and hate. Sometimes you can get out of control, lose your temper and say things that you don't mean. So if you don't mean what you say, where did it come from? Do you remember the tree of good and evil that God put in the garden of Eden and Adam and Eve took fruit from? Well, those same spirits are known to all mankind today. So the evil one, the devil was at work then, and he's trying to do the same today, influencing and causing trouble and pain in everyone's life.

He's just waiting for any opportunity to lie and blow things out of all proportion, splitting families and marriages, sometimes over nothing, as in Jacob's family. You will never get total control without an indwelling Christ in your life. Only by accepting Him, can you defeat the wiles of the devil, as Jesus did for you and me on the cross. Then you will have peace, love and reconciliation in your family. On this subject a salesman came to see me with a problem in his family, he explained that his eldest son was disrupting and causing trouble with the three younger children. The boy started to dress strangely and went quiet with his parents; they just couldn't talk to him. They asked him why he was behaving so badly and why he had changed so much, he was totally awkward and against anything his parents suggested, they just got silence from him, they were so worried. I told him it was a battle of love and hate and that he and his wife, through ignorance, were the instigators. He was shocked, saying 'How? Why? I love them all equally'. But I asked him, when was the last time he told his eldest boy that he loved him, took him anywhere, took an interest in what he was doing, gave him undivided attention, or gave him a hug, or some encouragement. I explained he was probably adding to the problem, by complaining about the boy's behaviour, putting him down, and telling him there's something wrong with him. In this young man's state, at fourteen years old, he hated his brothers and sisters, just as in Joseph's time. Nothing has changed. The eldest son was battling for the status he once had: the undivided love of his parents, and his brothers and sisters were in the way. They had now got what he had and still wanted, so love turned to hate. His father accepted what I said to him discouraged that he had got it so wrong. The truth had changed him in that moment from complaining about his son, to having such compassion for him. He just naturally wanted to run home and say sorry and give the boy a big hug. I told him to slow down, because it would take time to restore that love bond again, and that he would have to tiptoe or his son would back off. Anyway, some months passed and this man came to see me as usual about business, and I asked how his son was. He told me that initially his son had backed-off; but how he was able, gently, to give him more attention and time. Then he become excited and told me of a recent success in which the family was going out and the boy would not normally have gone with them. He said he would have been pleased he wasn't coming, because he would have spoiled the day, as usual. But things had since now changed and so he wanted him to come. And he came. His dad said, 'I can remember just putting my arm round my son's shoulder, walking across this field. You will never believe how I felt. That simple act and he allowed me to do it. We are now regaining that love and bond we had before'. His son was now laughing and smiling again and they were enjoying each other's company, I had to hold back the tears of joy. Father and son had changed from hate and conflict, to love and together-ness. Oh, such love, Simple, You can't buy it, and it's so pre-cious. The father did comment at the end of our conversation, that his son was still wearing those way-out clothes, but he said, 'I'm not concerned; I just have a laugh with him about it. It doesn't matter what's on the outside, it's what's on the inside that matters'. Thank you Jesus for your wisdom in this matter. The problems in this real life story are not typical in most famil-ies, but obviously they happen. It's a warning to some parents to watch the symptoms of kids going quiet, wearing black clothes, being disruptive, unfortunately some even commit suicide, all just to get at you, from as I'll show-you-attitude, instigated by the devil himself.

Righteousness, Wickedness

And Abraham drew near, and said, 'Wilt thou also destroy the righteous with the wicked'. (Gen 18:23)

In this scripture, Abraham is convening with God, asking him to intercede in the destruction of Sodom and Gomorra, to save the few righteous people living there. So God gave time for the righteous people to leave before the destruction of the wicked. The extent of wickedness was such that only one family walked away from that city alive. Wickedness like this is a reality today. How many cities in the world can you walk round and feel safe, particularly at night? So who is righteous? Who can you trust in any situation? The taxi driver? The police? The government? The holiday brochure? The stranger? The special offer? The builder? Newspapers? The doctor? The family? We even don't trust ourselves sometimes to make the right decision. Please don't get paranoid about who we can't trust, but if you think about it, who can you really trust? Not many, I guess. So the point I'm making, is as in Sodom and Gomorra, not many people today are completely righteous, or completely trustworthy.

So has society got safer and better? Has mankind made great leaps forward in the morality stakes? In the workplace for instance big brother is watching you; there are more managers and inspectors than workers in some places of work, and everyone is watching and checking on each other, because there is no trust any more. I have spoken to many people who used to be very efficient and enjoy their work, but who now find their job is pressurized with loads of useless paperwork, to justify themselves to the managers and inspectors. Many now hate their jobs and want to get out. Can you imagine how much it is costing? Billions of funds are wasted because the system is not righteous or programmed to trust, or to care about people. Who runs the system? It is the wicked one, the devil himself. And what are we doing to each other, allowing this to happen? You can't change the system; you can fight in it for righteousness, all your life, but I'm afraid that you will not change a thing in this wicked world, it is sealed, it's the domain of the devil. The only thing you can do is to come out of it and live in another place – no, it's not your dream of a desert island where you think you will have peace and tranquility away from other people, because you would take your worldly and wicked contamination with you in your thoughts, your baggage would be full of it. The devil loves isolation where he can have a field-day undisturbed in your thoughts, persecuting you, where there is no-one around to share your thoughts with as you lie disillusioned in so-called paradise, with nothing to do, but to listen to the persecuting words within your own mind, because you are still in and of this world. It is written that if you first seek the kingdom of God and his righteousness, then all things will be given unto you – all things worth while, that is.

So instead of your isolation, come out of this wicked world into the divine protection of the kingdom of God, which is not of this world, where all your thoughts and fears will be vanquished. Come into the safety of the kingdom where Jesus awaits you, not to change this world externally, but to change you personally from the inside. He will come into you as your only divine protector from the wicked wiles of the devil, so stop dwelling on the bad news of this world, but take on the good news of Jesus Christ. Then, only then, could you personally make a difference, and a kingdom example in this world. Amen.

Disciplining children

Chasten your son while there is hope, and let not thy soul spare for his crying. (Proverbs 19:18)

Foolishness is bound in the heart of a child; but the rod of correction shall drive it far from him. (Proverbs 22:15)

The scriptures above instructs us to discipline our child unto righteousness while they are young, even if they are crying, because if you don't it's too late when they are in their teens, as they will not listen and will do their own wicked things not yours. Kids only know what you have taught them. It's the parent's responsibility, so please don't let it be too late for you. Let me give you an example of a simple instruction to a child today that is not adhered to: No doesn't mean no any more, not only to the child, but also to the parent. Many parents are themselves insecure, so they spoil their children, buying them everything they want. It's called an insecure love, thinking if they don't give the children everything they ask for, they won't love them. The child invariably then grows up without respect for their parents and treats them with contempt, which is wicked. If then they can't get what they want, or do what they want, or say what they want, they use emotional blackmail stamping their feet, shouting obscenities, and the like. You may wonder why they are treating you like this, since you have given them everything they wanted. Sadly though you did do so, it was for the wrong reason. You got it wrong. So as a parent you can create a wicked child, through ignorance, or sometimes because of how you were brought up, living from problem to problem. Yes, you worked hard and slaved to give your child everything you never had; you gave up so much of your time and even life, for your children. But do you think they realize that? Or were you just used and taken for granted and now they are so hard-hearted, that they criticise you and tell you how to live your life, the life you gave up for them. Perhaps I paint a poor picture, but I'm afraid is it one which is typical today. There is not much stability with kids today, so that you notice well-behaved kids immediately, because they are rare. What are we doing to our kids, as we spoil them rotten? A friend has recently said that kids get so much, they don't know when it is Christmas any more. We are amusing ourselves to death. This is part of the truth of creation, look what we are creating. Prisons are not emptying, on the contrary they are getting fuller. This world now promotes tolerance to the degree of insanity, particularly in my country, England. Jesus said.

> As many as I love, I rebuke and chasten: be zealous therefore and repent. (Rev 3:19)

> My son, despise not the chastening of the Lord; neither be weary of His correction. (Proverbs 3:11)

> Before I was afflicted I went astray: but now I have kept thy word. (Psalm 119:67)

> He that spareth his rod hateth his son: but he that loveth him chasteneth him betimes. (Peter 13:24)

> Withhold not correction from the child: for if thou beatest him with the rod, he shall not die. (Peter 23:13)

> Foolishness is bound in the heart of a child; but the rod of correction shall drive it far from him. (Peter 22:15)

Parental duties are described in Scripture,

Train up a child in the way he should go: and when he is old, he will not depart from it. (Peter 22:6)

I have given much Scripture on the discipline of children, because they are the next generation, oh what hope have they got, it's that important that God tells us, if we don't discipline our children we must hate them. Afflicted above means discipline, so discipline your child and stand firm if you love them, teach them what is right, or righteous. It never hurt me when I was young. You know it makes sense.

The question I asked earlier is who can you really trust, to guard and guide you in all righteousness. The answer to that is it's Jesus Christ. Otherwise, you can follow the world of the devil and peer-pressure, unto wickedness. Talking about rules in schools, the rules and regulations about teachers being left with a child on their own, it's protectionism gone mad, the teachers have been vetted, so where is the danger? It's from the kids! The teachers walk round with handcuffs on because all they can do is send the naughty children into another class, or sometimes have them suspended. The government has put so much pressure into education, thinking that's the answer to all life's ills, looking at the stats, more children are taking drugs and at a younger age, there were no ASBOs a few years ago. There are more kids truanting, gangs and the like. Why do the kids have to be taught how to interact with each other, to be kind and help one another and how to play games in the play ground?) Remember it's called a play ground – but the kids don't know how to play any more, they just go round intimidating each other). There has to be a strict discipline, or they would get no respect from the children and there would be chaos in the classroom. What are we doing to our kids, giving them rights and weapons beyond reason? And who are these people behind all these rules who keep changing their minds about how to teach our children? They keep changing their minds because they keep getting it wrong. Teachers don't know if they are coming are going. The balance has tipped too far the wrong way. Teachers now need protection from the kids, and have to spend more time on discipline, than doing what they are paid to do – teach the kids. Some children are brought up feeling inferior or superior in the system. It's obvious that we can't all be born with the same intelligence or memory level; but the system still labels our kids good, bad, or thick, which is disgusting. I always brought up my kids to believe that if they have done their best, they have passed, irrespective of the result. I ask you what is society doing to our kids? They are our future, and it's not their fault. A disciplined child is a happy child, because it knows where it stands and knows right from wrong; and this gives peace in your home, laughter and joy, instead of conflict. It's the parents' responsibility whether their child grows up righteous or wicked. Ask yourself, if children are born innocent what goes wrong? Different circumstances can steer a child to do and think wrong things by influences outside the family, as it did in mine, it's crucial that you try and keep your child away from 'the wrong crowd'. If you get good grounding as a child in what is right, through discipline, your parents loving you righteously, it will give you a good chance of not succumbing to wicked temptations. If you are one of these children, please thank your parents for their love and sacrifice, because it isn't easy saying 'No', to your wanting, for your sake. There are many things you will not understand as a child, indeed until you have your own children. So if you want divine protection and guidance to what is righteous, whatever state you are in, Jesus Christ is the answer to an overwhelming joy in your family. Parents enjoy and love your children. Children: enjoy and love your parents. To finish this on a good note, here are a few poems thankful children wrote to a teacher, before leaving their school.

The greatest teacher in the world
Always happy never sad, helps us out when we are feeling bad,
Forever happy smiling away, helps us out knows what to say,
She is the sunshine in the rain; she's always smiling never in pain,
Clapping and dancing where ever she goes, skipping and singing
    on her hands and her toes,
All the children are clever, our teachers the best ever, I'll really miss
    you want to stay here forever.

Miss you've taught me maths, English and art,
You've touched the top, bottom and centre of my heart,
I've learned over quite a long and happy while,
How to make you happy, laugh and smile,
You've picked me to do stuff that was really great,
You're not just a teacher; you are my very best mate,
We all went to Filey I was selfish and said I didn't want to stay,
But you hugged me and said, 'It's okay',
You've looked after me like one of your own
My fondness for you has grown and grown,
You're part of my family in a special kind of way,
I wish that with you I could joyfully stay,
You've helped me with friends and now I have more,
You led me to the future you're a shining star,
You've lent me a very big helping hand,
For you I would not trade even a million grand,
I'm not entering the big wide world just yet,
But the help you've given me to get there I won't forget.
If teachers were flowers I'd pick you the most beautiful lily glowing
    above all others.

Thank you for always being there for me, when things have gone
wrong.

    You have been the best teacher I have ever had and thank you for
being there for me with sats. Like you were saying, I have done well
all through the year. Well I wouldn't have been able to do it without
you. You have helped me a very lot with my life; I will really miss
you when I leave.

This letter written by a mum.

> Just a little something to wear on a Saturday afternoon, [this was all my son's idea], he wanted to get something extra special for an extra special teacher.
>
> Having you as my son's teacher this year has boosted his confidence within himself and confidence in his ability to work hard and succeed. This would not have been possible without the hard work and dedication of such a magnificent teacher. The support, encouragement and opportunities that you have given my son to progress and succeed through PE. Have been greatly appreciated by my son. To be chosen to compete in football and athletics and represent his school has made my son proud. In this year with you, my son has enjoyed getting to know his teacher through your chats about football and sport, especially when you have shown interest in his own football development. Thank you for everything. You are a star!

These letters are about positive changes that have taken place in these children's lives, appreciated by them so much that they want to express it by writing it down. The teacher didn't give them any worldly goods, she just showed genuine care and guidance, through discipline and it cost nothing. Are you listening parents? It's you they want, not what you give them.

Truth and Lies

The opposite of lying and deceit, is honesty and truthfulness. One state cannot exist without the other, it's impossible. A good example of lying in Scripture is

Genesis 27:19: 'And Jacob said unto his father, "I am Esau thy first-born"'; And again Isaac asking Jacob in Genesis 27:24: '"And he said, art thou my very son Esau?" And he said, "I am"'.

So Jacob lied and deceived his father Isaac into believing he was his brother Esau. Isaac was only deceived because he was blind and of old age. His mother took full advantage of this by playing her part in the deceit, because Jacob was her favourite. So Jacob received from Isaac his father's blessing, which belonged to Esau the first born, because he (Jacob) wanted the blessing and inheritance.

A modern-day example might be the Iraq war. Did we go to war because Iraq had weapons of mass destruction or had they made their minds up that they were going to war no matter what? Was it about oil, or was it to bring Saddam to justice for his crimes against humanity? Did they lie, or not? You see the system tells us to go soft on discipline at home and generally in society; then takes thousands of innocent lives of people (on both sides). What a terrible cost. They can't get it right at home, so for some reason want to interfere in other people's countries and affairs.

A few years before, a girl was preparing to go to work, dressed immaculately, perfumed and the like. She worked at the White House. Because of her, the president was brought down, just the same as Saddam. But this time there were no bullets, rockets, aircraft carriers, jet fighters, money wasted and loss of life; the only 'missiles' were those she caught on her attire. Then because of DNA the truth of the sexual scandal was realized. I personally have the utmost sympathy with the president, because one of the most dangerous temptations to man is woman and vice versa. Just as in Jacob's time, there are questions we can ask: Did she plan it? Did she know his weakness? Was it a conspiracy? And why didn't she naturally wash the dress, as others would do? So where are the morals in these true-life stories of truth and lies? The circumstances were and are certainly different. Two presidents were brought down, one with a massive loss of life and financial cost, the other red lipstick, a nice revealing dress, perfume and the like, but no lives and no cost. Doesn't it make you wonder about who is really powerful on this earth? You see, in all these cases there were plans to deceive and to lie for gain. In these examples, the opposites expose each other; you cannot have a lie without the truth, or vice versa. In these examples of giving-in to the tempter, to the devil himself, to sin, you suffer in your sin as do everyone around you – your family and friends. God made sure in creation that everyone suffers in sin, because of love, or we would never learn. Some think they have got away with it all their lives, but hell will get than in the end. Only through Jesus will you have the power to tell the truth all the time, and to have peace. So position or money, even royalty cannot save you from your sin and being found out, just as in Bible times. Only Jesus the saviour can forgive your sins, as He did mine, giving you a new life and a chance to change your life. It's a reality that some people will never forgive you for your past, doing the devil's work for him, or giving you a chance to change, these people condemn you forever, with no forgiveness. These people don't realize, in their bitterness, that they are condemned already in their unforgiveness, and that's the truth.

A Stranger

> And when the sun was going down, a deep sleep fell on Abraham; and lo, an horror of great darkness fell upon him. (Gen 15:12)

> And he said unto Abraham, know of a surety that thy seed shall be a stranger in the land that is not theirs, and shall serve them four hundred years. (Gen 15:13)

This is God foretelling Abraham that his people one day that they will be strangers in a land that is not theirs, which is Egypt. Do you remember the story of God's promise that he would bring them out of that land, to the Promised Land, using Moses as the leader and instrument of God? I tell you, the truth is today, yes even as you read these words, that by Jesus, and only by Him, can you enter the promised land. This land is heaven on earth. I ask you, how many more years do you want to be a stranger, a slave, as in Egypt, a wanderer, a fugitive, a stranger to the word of God and to life itself? You may think within yourself, my life is OK; but I tell you even from my own experience there is more to life than coming and going, life and death, going along with yet not belonging, just existing in this world. You are obviously here for a while, but you can be a stranger, blinded from reality and truth of God while you are temporarily here. You can live a lie while you are here, and you might never know the truth of this promised land, knowing and having a real purpose of why you and I live.

Let me give you another example of being isolated from the truth and living a lie. An explorer comes to an undiscovered land where the people practice cannibalism. He tells them it is wrong to do that. They reply, 'It's all we know', so for them it's right. They have never before been told it's wrong and they are ignorant of the truth, in their isolation. In their state they lived a lie; but it was only revealed as such when measured against truth. We too, if we shut Jesus from our lives, we too will never know the truth of why we exist. You could still be in the jungle of this world, a stranger, void of the truth. I know I have also been in the jungle experience of life, where I thought I'd got life worked all out, but God our creator has brought me into His glorious light, from that dark jungle.

> And this is the condemnation, that light is come into the world, and men loved darkness rather than light, because their deeds were evil. For everyone that doeth evil hateth the light, lest his deeds should be reproved. But he that doeth truth cometh to the light that his deeds may be made manifest, that they are wrought in God. (John 3:19–21)

You don't know you are in it, until you come out of it, where you can see more clearly. God clears a new path of life from the jungle for us into His glorious light and to a reward of eternal life with Him. Alleluia.

I encourage you no matter what experience you are having in this world I call a jungle. Jesus is waiting for you to call out to Him, 'Jesus help me a sinner'. He is waiting for your call. Don't be a stranger to life itself. Go on call and open your heart to the truth of creation. He will never let you down. Amen.

Materialism

So man like an eager beaver, with a discovery mindset and making more and more things, are you happier, have you more peace, has it quieted the ills of your life? No. Man has to keep his sanity, to keep pushing on, or he gets bored with his own existence. The human mind needs to be fed with something, or anything, it's a frustrating life looking for temporary enjoyment, nothing permanent, always looking to satisfy our yearning to fill that void, with gadgets and new things. A lot of people simply rely on the television too much, some take drugs and alcohol for satisfaction, taking their mind to another place; because they are bored with their own existence in this world. They are dead, looking for life in materialism, looking for a new kick. All the fantastic things we have made, will never satisfy your wanting, or our souls, nothing that we see with our eyes can ever give us permanent satisfaction, only satisfaction for a while. To truly satisfy this perplexed generation there is only that blessed assurance of Jesus Christ, He who came to set an example that we might follow; only then and through Him can we get satisfaction for our souls.

Let's consider humankind's life of materialistic striving with the life of creatures in the animal Kingdom. Let's take a cow for example: it doesn't change its diet. It speaks the same language. It never complains. It knows how to reproduce. It doesn't cause trouble, nor is it aggressive. It's satisfied, It hasn't diverted from why it was created, and it doesn't have to put it's own species in prison. Doesn't it make you wonder why the animals are happier and more content than us.

The reason we aren't like the cow is that we are made in God's image of good and evil. The cow wasn't. God sent the knowledge of good and evil that was from Him to earth.

For God so loved the world, that he gave his only begotten son, that whosoever believeth in him should not perish, but have everlasting life. (John 3:16)

So why don't we do as scripture says and live our lives properly? The cow is happy doing what it was created to do So why don't we be like the cow and conform to what we are created for, to follow in the footsteps of Jesus Christ and His word, having that same contentment. You know it makes sense.

Man is in an ever decreasing circle, a prisoner in his mind, he is wrapped up in himself, lost in materialism, always wants, never satisfied. If you follow Jesus He will put you on a straight road to heaven, instead of that circle which goes nowhere, but which is hell on earth. It's as though on judgment day, you sit there feeling guilty and you are searching for excuses in your mind, for your sin, but it's too late, they come to drag you away to put you into hell fire and death. But then this man comes forward, saying, 'Take me instead. I will pay the price for their sin'. That man is Jesus Christ who paid the price for the whole world; he wants to die in your place for your sin. Such love. So come to him and be forgiven. Start again. Stop taking the drugs of this world. It's never too late. Please come. God gives you another chance, as He did me. Take it. Please don't waste the sacrifice that He made for you.

He that loveth not knoweth not God; for God is love. In this was manifested the love of God towards us, because God sent his only begotten Son into the world, that we might live through him. Herein is love, not that we loved God, but that he loved us, and sent his son to be the propitiation for our sins. Beloved, if God so loved us, we ought also to love one another. (1 John 4:8 – 11)

Who being the brightness of his glory, and the express image of his person, and upholding all things by the word of his power, when he had by himself purged our sins, sat down on the right hand of the Majesty on high. (Hebrews 1:3) Amen.

Humanity

Let me give you a few fascinating facts about ourselves – human beings. This information is well documented, in science and biological literature for all to see, but I feel it is an advantage and food for thought for the reader considering the truth of creation. We are made up of trillions of atoms and assembled in a manner to create you and me. The atoms don't know us, or know of their own existence. They don't even care about us, but obligingly they are put together by God perfectly in creation. If you were able to pick them off one-by-one, you would be a pile of dust, as God said in Scripture,

> In the sweat of thy face shall though eat bread, till thou return unto the ground; for out of it wast thou taken: for dust thou art, and unto dust shalt thou return. (Gen 3:19)

If you look on a bottle of vitamin tablets you will see a list of ingredients. I'm not going to list them all, but there's, iron, copper, salt, zinc, potassium, water . . . all of which can do us good. From a creation view point, it amazes me what nutrients we need from the earth to live a healthy and full life. Where do they come from, I wonder? Will they run out? Once again marvel at the planning of our creator God who was able to envisage what we needed from the beginning. Only such a creator God would know and provide for all our needs, or there would no point creating anything. Can you just try to imagine before men entered this world, God put everything on earth that we needed, down to every last vitamin. It's obvious that our bodies need protein for example. But it is impossible for man to make protein – which comes from amino acids. Not only that, man can't make it, because it makes itself, spontaneously, without direction, so the chance of us making it is nil. The eye has 40,000 nerve endings and receptors, to give you colour. Even Charles Darwin in his theories of evolution had to admit that the eye itself cannot come from natural selection. So the evolution theory is out of the window in that respect.

Natural selection is, as most have seen on the television wild life programmes, a pecking order, in which only the strongest animal in each species breeds, and so the species is sustained. If the weakest bred the species would go downhill, degenerate and die out. Don't you think that that's amazing?

> And God said, Let the earth bring forth the living creature after his kind, cattle, and creeping things, and beasts of the earth after his kind: and it was so. (Gen 1:24)

Kind in this scripture means species. Within the species you can get different mutations and colours as in animals and man, but you can't cross over, you can't inter-breed between species, if we or they could, we would have millions of different kinds on earth, it would be freakish and horrendous, with no end. For example, if man came from monkeys, why can't we inter-breed with them? We know it doesn't work; but if we were of the same species it would work. So this proves that we didn't evolve from monkeys. Man is so fickle that he looked at the nearest look-alike and said we come from them and then tried to prove it. So why do we, so-called superior, humans just assume that we came from monkeys? It's more feasible that monkeys came from us in our degenerative society! At least they are not destroying the earth and each other, because of a 'got-to-have' mentality. Monkeys have from the beginning of time been satisfied with their lot, let's look at them and learn from their simplicity. Lucky for us that we have a God, who knew all this in the beginning, and gave and separated all species. Scientists have discovered a different blueprint in our DNA which makes it impossible to cross species or kind naturally. So the evolution theory is wrong, not just on this one point that I am making, but scientist's own deeper studies which show that it is wrong and it is now common knowledge in their circles to be impossible. Don't you think reader that God at the time of creation, amazingly put this programming unseen in all living things, of which there are millions of species, so there wouldn't be an inter-breeding free for all? It just blows my mind. What a God.

My youngest daughter is an embryologist and she tells me that it is a miracle anyone gets pregnant. She says that mathematically, there are more than eight million possible chromosome combinations for each egg and sperm. If each parent has this many combinations, then one couple could produce more than 7×10^{13} offspring with different combinations of parental chromosome. It is also amazing that the sperm has to have a tail to swim to reach the egg, which gives off a chemical to attract the sperm. When one sperm reaches the egg and fertilisation takes place, it causes a reaction in the egg, which releases granules from its periphery. This causes a chemical alteration in the egg's protective coat; it goes hard which renders it impenetrable to other sperm, to stop more than one sperm getting in. Atoms, chemicals and cells etc. cannot be and are nothing without the other and can only exist within a membrane. The point I'm making with these facts is that they must have all come together and created together, so the evolution theory is impossible. I hope the reader found these few facts interesting.

Free will

On many occasions, Christians say 'You need God in your life'. It seems to me many people are in denial of who God is; they should say you need Jesus in your life. Every person (and I mean everyone) has got God in their lives, simply because God made man in His image, I'm sorry to quote this scripture from Genesis 3:5 again to make my point,

> For God doth know that in the day ye eat thereof, then your eyes will be opened, and ye shall be as God's, knowing good and evil.

So every one of us are as mini gods walking and living on this earth with the knowledge of good and evil, made in His image, physically and spiritually we are like Him, it's not possible to be anything else, but like him in every way. You see in the beginning man took from both sides of God spiritually that is and is still with us today, good and evil. The key word is knowledge of good and evil, in other words you know of it, but knowing doesn't determine whether you are a good or bad person, unless you act or think upon either. So we are open to doctrine of all spirits good or bad. What determines who you are, is whether your thoughts, life and actions are one or the other, or in between, or a mixture in your life. So who are you? Are you a bad person, living to an evil influence of sin, tempted by the devil? He's always looking for recruits to hell. Or are you a good person and I don't mean your account of goodness, I mean God's goodness. Only through Jesus Christ, he who represents the righteousness of God can you receive. God didn't put you in a straightjacket, He gave you a free will to choose how to live your life and look after our environment. Without the opposite you would have no free will to choose because there would be nothing to choose from. Some people blame God for numerous things that happen in the world and in their personal life, I say look at your personal choices, don't blame God when you choose wrong.

Money

God didn't make planes, trains, cars, intending them to crash. He didn't tell people to rob and kill each other for gain. And He didn't build buildings below the water level, or on fault lines. God didn't pollute this beautiful world with filth. God didn't tell man to cut corners and put money before people, creating pressure in all our lives throughout the world. No, we did; and the result is suffering. Yes, we make each other suffer, because of our greed. Can somebody tell me why are we doing this to each other in a so-called civilized country, where we are not safe in hospital because of inadequate hygiene; when we had to kill our cows and sheep, feeding them stuff they weren't created by God to eat, and people died, yes people are dying, because we are putting money before anything. This is why God says,

For the love of money is the root of all evil. (Timothy 6:10)

It's getting worse. Why? Reader, look for yourself: Why is money the first consideration when you are ill, and not your health? Doctors have gone to court recently to ask permission not to resuscitate a child when needed, because in their opinion the child is not worth saving. To save money they wanted to purposely let it die. Where are we going? What are we doing? Who are these people who want power over life and death? Thank God the parents loved their child unconditionally and, can you believe it, they fought the doctors in court for their own child's life. Thank God they won. The child is now safe at home with its loving parents.

Money puts powerful lights in shop windows, particularly in jewelers' shops. The butcher has special lights to make the meat look redder. There is a sale on permanently in some shops, it seems. I've known closing-down sales go on for years. Just look at the adverts on the television. Who are these people behind these adverts? Reader, have a look for yourselves. I just shake my head in disgust when I think what lengths these people stoop to, just to sell a packet of soap powder. They are an insult to our intelligence.

Money puts girls on street corners. Money puts people in prison. Money destroys lives with drugs. Money creates illicit trafficking of people – and we thought that we are now civilized and slavery is no more. Money pressurises everyone at work, because we are all answerable to someone. That is why, when people ask me what was the best thing about working for myself, I would answer, 'It is the freedom from people pressure. I'm not answerable to anyone; only to myself.' But ultimately, of course I must answer to Jesus. Money tells you how you should look. Money tells you what to wear, or what's in fashion. Money tells you to pierce your body. Money tells you to decorate your body with tattoos, even where they can never be seen. I wonder if people with tattoos know something I don't know; maybe they sleep better or something with a tattoo. Money tells you you should by a new pair of jeans with holes in because it's fashionable. When we were kids, if we had holes in our trousers we would be classed as poor and everybody would laugh at us. The world's gone mad. Yes, mad about fashion. Tongues in; tongues out – on trainers that is. Fasten your shoe laces; don't fasten your shoe laces. I wonder who was the first person not to fasten their shoe laces. Now wear your underclothes on top with jeans. Now make sure your top is short enough to show the pin in your bellybutton. Now don't you just look great? What a mix! Look folks. Look, look at my pin. Don't I just look great?

Just a minute, everybody who is anybody has got one now. In fact you all look the same. Can somebody tell me if the pin in your belly button adds one little jot to your life? Oh it's wicked. I'm scratching my head again and wondering why I am getting bald. It's enough to pull your hair out.

Aren't we just like sheep gone astray when we follow the world's manipulating system?

Who do you think controls the world's system, and who screws the lid even tighter? It is Satan himself, who controls your decisions and life in this world's system. Come to Jesus and make proper choices in your life. You know it makes sense.

> Love not the world, neither the things that are in the world. If any man love the world, the love of the Father is not in him. For all that is in the world, the lust of the flesh, and the lust of the eyes, and the pride of life, is not of the Father, but is of the world. And the world passeth away, and the lust thereof: but he that doeth the will of God abideth forever. (1 John 2: 15–17)

I have given you a few examples of the worldly system, and scripture above. It's not the physical world that's against God. It's the sinful system that we are in and go along with; the system that controls you and your decisions as in the everyday examples about what you wear; what you do; what you think. That's why, as Christians say, we are in the world, but not of it; not of the system. Don't complain when people and this world let you down. The system is not programmed to care. It will just get you into debt. It's dishonest. So don't put your confidence in things, because the system will tell you they are no good anymore, they are out of date, you are too old, you waste good money on the system. You pay into the system but the system will let you down. Wealth is uncertain. But God is sure and solid and reliable. Jesus himself was tempted by Satan, who controls the world's system. Jesus said,

> Then saith Jesus unto him, Get thee hence, Satan: for it is written, Thou shalt worship the Lord thy God, and him only shalt thou serve. (Matthew 4:10)

So who are you serving? Is it the robber, or the rewarder?

Self

How does God want me to live? What should I do when I get up of a morning? Scripture says,

> This I say then, 'Walk in the Spirit, and ye shall not fulfill the lust of the flesh. For the flesh lusteth against the spirit, and the spirit against the flesh: and these are contrary the one to the other: so that ye cannot do the things that ye would'. (Galatians 5:16-17)

> Watch and pray that ye enter not into temptation: the spirit indeed is willing, but the flesh is weak. (Matthew 26:41)

I tell you the truth every day is a battle for your sanity. Nothing in particular or of importance might be happening in your life, but you don't feel good without the truth of God's creation in your life. You don't know why, if you have no understanding of the life you live. The battle is within you, in your thoughts, as in the Scriptures above. The spirit is against the flesh? So what is the flesh? It's you, living selfishly, unto yourself. Self cannot forgive. It is negative, self-centred, carries guilt, worries, dwells on past hurts, judges others, makes comparison with others, has no joy, it is defensive, bitter, anxious, etc. As God puts it in Scripture,

> Now the works of the flesh are manifest, which are these; adultery, fornication, uncleanness, lasciviousness, Idolatry, witchcraft, hatred, variance, emulations, wrath, strife, seditions, heresies, envying, murders, drunkenness, reveling, and such like: of which

I tell you before, as I have also told you in time past, that they which do such things shall not inherit the kingdom of God. (Galatians 5:19–21)

What a list. So let me give you an example: You can have your thoughts on self, for any of the reasons listed above, which makes you sad, or worse. Then, if you concentrate on your work, your colleagues, your children or grandchildren, or anything, or anyone other than yourself, doing good, helping or just considering others . . . As your thoughts move from your self (flesh), notice how much better you feel. It's in the quiet times when the devil, in your thoughts, robs you of your peace. He only brings up the bad things. He remind you of your past, tells you, you are never going to cope that the future's bleak, with nothing to look forward to. But remember, the devil is the father of all lies. He was a liar from the beginning and is speaking to your flesh life. Self. If you live the lie (lies don't exist in reality) you don't exist because your whole life is a lie. There is no point in your existence. In this position the devil has got you just where he wants you. If you live a totally unselfish life, sacrificed, your flesh life is dead. You cannot be robbed by the devil any more. You take nothing from this world so why live according to it?

So, how can I live in the spirit of Jesus Christ, instead of by the flesh?

Romans 12:1–2 say, 'I beseech you therefore, brethren, by the mercies of God, that ye present your bodies a living sacrifice, holy acceptable to God, which is your reasonable service. And be not conformed to this world: but be ye transformed by the renewing of your mind, that ye may prove what is that good, and acceptable, and perfect, will of God'.

So, in this scripture Paul is saying sacrifice your life, which is reasonable. God doesn't make a big deal about it. It's just reasonable. In other words, there is a good reason for it. If you have died to self, your mind is not thinking of self. It's impossible. So, automatically your mind is renewed and is only thinking of others, which means you can't be robbed by the devil's lies any more. Let me tell you a story. A friend of mine, who I've known for about fifteen years, who's (not) a Christian and has never wanted to know, out of the blue last week, asked me, 'How should I live my life'? We were having a game of snooker at the time. But I just lay on the floor with my arms across my chest and said to him, 'What am I doing?' He said, 'You're being dead', I said, 'Well that's how God wants you to live your life'. I explained, that when you are dead to self, people can kick you, spit on you, call you names, hate you, lie to you, be critical, unkind, angry, steal from you etc., but they can't hurt you because you are dead to self. No-one can hurt a dead person. Now, if you are dead to self (which is sin and the system) Jesus can fill that void in your life. Where is Jesus? He is in heaven, sinless, raised from the dead. So you too will be raised from your living death on earth, living a heavenly life on earth, as a sinless servant of God, glorifying Him and speaking the gospel to the world. In this position you have the full armour of God on. Nothing can penetrate it. It's impossible. What a life. Alleluia.

> But the fruit of the Spirit is love, joy, peace, longsuffering, gentleness, goodness, faith, meekness, temperance: against such there is no law. And they that are Christ's have crucified the flesh with the affections and lusts. If we live in the Spirit, let us also walk in the Spirit. Let us not be desirous of vain glory, provoking one another, envying one another. (Galatians 5:22–26)

I feel it's good to give examples. Jesus was the ultimate example, you can witness and see the fruits above through sacrifices, which speak louder than words. In my testimony, I speak of a man who had robbed me after I had given him financial help. Instead of hating him or dismissing him I put my arms round him and told him that I still loved him and I could still help him. Now, self, flesh, could not have done that. Self would have wanted him locked up. Self would have wanted to bring to the attention of others of how wonderful I was and how I had been let down. Self would have been angry and would have given him a dressing-down. Self could have hated and not forgiven him affecting the rest of my life. Self would have only helped him in the first place for vanity. Or, self would not have helped him at all. I would have done any these things for the sake of my flesh. But I didn't, because I had sacrificed my flesh. I was dead to self, the circumstance could not hurt me, because I was living in the spirit of Jesus Christ. I had given up living for money and ultimately living for myself. It was not the old me any more: it was Jesus in me, setting me free still to love this man, and to forgive him. The robber of life, the devil, could not touch me, because he can only operate in the world's system, or the flesh, if you are dead to both, fear of death is vanquished, because you are dead already, you can't die twice, and you now live in the kingdom of God, which is not of this world's system, but separate and safe, forever. I can tell you, reader, truly: you have heaven on earth and eternal life with your saviour Jesus Christ your divine protector. Believe and be saved.

Above all, taking the shield of faith, wherewith ye shall be able to quench all the fiery darts of the wicked. (Ephesians 6:16)

I would like to give you a few examples from the Bible of mighty men of faith, who show that selfishness cannot prevail.

Moreover he kissed all his brethren, and wept upon them: and after that his brethren talked with him. (Genesis 45:15)

This is the story of Joseph whose brothers had sold him into slavery because they hated him. When they met up many years later he not only forgave them he kissed and wept upon them, creating reconciliation, sowing good for evil. Self could not have done it; self would have wanted recompense. That's where the devil operates, in self, in hate, creating division. Reader, I encourage you to look at your life's virtues. Are they right with God? Do you hate? Or are you unforgiving, even of yourself? Look to Jesus to help you in the endeavours of your life. Fight the good fight of faith towards God through Jesus Christ. Joseph then spoke later to his brothers,

> And Joseph said unto them, 'Fear not: for I am in the place of God. But as for you, ye thought evil against me; but God meant it unto good, to bring to pass, as it is this day, to save much people alive. Now therefore fear ye not: I will nourish you, and your little ones'. And he comforted them, and spake kindly unto them. (Genesis 50:19–21)

In this Scripture Joseph's words kicked the devil into touch. Twice, he said, Fear not to address his brothers' guilty fear, explaining it was in God's plan what they had done, which comforted them and he was kind to them. Again in this explanation Joseph recognised that his brothers felt uncomfortable around him, because of their sin, but he put them at ease. He wanted to comfort them, creating a solid and true reconciliation that would last. Who was he thinking about? He was thinking of them and not his selfish self. Alleluia.

Another example of unselfishness in Scripture is in

> And they stoned Stephen, calling upon God, and saying, 'Lord Jesus, receive my spirit'. And he kneeled down, and cried with a loud voice, 'Lord, lay not this sin to their charge'. And when he had said this, he fell asleep. (Acts 7:59–60)

Reader, I shake my head, it's hard to write about such a man of God. Oh, to be in that same place in God through Jesus Christ. Stephen, a spirit-filled business man, not even thinking of his own life as he was being stoned to death, because he was dead already in the Lord. Can you imagine that place? Can you? In which his strength was secured in his earlier sacrifice of self; he was dead already but alive in Jesus and in his life he had already been raised from the death of his old life – born again. Only from this place can you live your destiny now, a heavenly life already. Can you only think of others, even the stone-throwers, in asking God to forgive them, as they actually stoned him? Wow. He was innocent, but because of his power-ful preaching of Jesus Christ, not of himself, because self wasn't there, they killed him. I ask you, reader, to contemplate the scene. Were self or flesh evident? He knew in his heart that he was already in a better place. They couldn't hurt him, because he was dead to self already. You can't die twice, or hurt a dead person. He said,

Lord Jesus receive my spirit.

Amen.

Similar to Stephen, Paul rose from the death of his old life. In Acts 14:19–20 we read

And there came thither certain Jews from Antioch and Iconium, who persuaded the people, and, having stoned Paul, drew him out of the city, supposing he had been dead. Howbeit, as the disciples stood round about him, he rose up, and came into the city.

Paul having been stoned because of his belief, was thrown out of the city. They thought he was dead, but, obviously, he was only unconscious, because when he came round, he walked back into the city. Would self have walked back into the city?

No, self would have run a mile. Paul's life was totally unselfish after his conversion, his strength in Christ was the difference. From being a persecutor of Christians, he became a Christian. From being one who stoned Christians he was stoned himself. Once he threw Christians into prison, then he was thrown into prison himself. You see, you don't know the difference, until you've received the difference. And we, as servants, must show this difference to the world in our new life. I can identify slightly with Paul, as I had forty three years in the world's system. I know of the immense difference as Paul did, calling his old life dung in comparison to the new one – you can't say it stronger than that! He persecuted Christians and instigated their punishment. He was even present at Stephen's death and went along with it. But Jesus intervened on the Damascus road. Jesus, totally changed Paul's life, so that he went on to write much of the New Testament in the Bible. What a transformation. Do you, reader, want to be transformed into a better heavenly life? Jesus is waiting for your call.

Another example from Paul's life in Philippi, recorded in

> And when they had laid many stripes upon them, they cast them into prison, charging the jailer to keep them safely who, having received such a charge, thrust them into the inner prison, and made their feet fast in the stocks. And at midnight Paul and Silas prayed, and sang praises unto God. (Acts 16:23–25)

They had bean beaten up, thrown into prison, locked in the stocks, and it was pitch black because they were in the inner prison. Were they crying, feeling sorry for them selves? No, they were singing. Could self sing in prison? No, self was dead. They had given up their lives already. They couldn't consider their selfish selves. So they could be happy in any circumstance, and so could you dear reader. You can't feel a thing when you have sacrificed your life unto Jesus. It sets you free to love and consider others only. Note that, in fact, later in Scripture the jailer, '. . . brought them out, and said,

> 'Sirs, what must I do to be saved?' And they said, 'Believe on the Lord Jesus Christ, and thou shalt be saved, and thy house'. (Acts 16:30–31)

Alleluia. Paul explains his joy in tribulation,

> Therefore I take pleasure in infirmities, in reproaches, in necessities, in persecutions, in distresses for Christ's sake: for when I am weak, then I am strong. (2 Cor 12:10)

Ask yourself, why should we live our lives with ups and downs which are just within our own mind? Why not have an even keel in your life whether you are at work or play or on holiday? Paul says he takes pleasure in the downs, because he doesn't live to them any more, instead he lives for Jesus who paid the ultimate price for his (and our) ups and downs. He paid it in full with His life, showing how we should live too, through sacrifice of self. We are set free with no more hurts, so we can even smile and sing as Paul did if we are in prison. So, let's kick-down the restrictive prison gates down in our lives and be set free in the truth of Jesus Christ and receive a free eternal holiday, by living for Christ instead of our hurting selves. Amen.

Jesus

After I was saved, it used to dismay me to find mere buildings called churches and to see men's names on such buildings. This was not right. God's people are the church, not buildings. And I tell you there is only one church, that of Jesus Christ who is its chief cornerstone. How can man put any name on God's house? Those people were mighty in God, only because Christ died on the cross for them, and transformed their lives. They didn't preach the gospel in their own name but in the name of Jesus; because the gospel was His not theirs. So why glorify man? I would imagine if these men were here today, they would rip their own names down from these buildings. The sad thing is that the powers that be in these organizations will carry on sinning and change nothing. I can confess that nothing will change in their organization in the things of God. They will go downhill and never be blessed unless they repent and change their ways. Come on, listen you people. Get out of the cold organization mode. It's a relationship. You can't relate to others or stay together (as in marriage) without a relationship. God needs you in the kingdom, not in the rudiments of this physical world. The ultimate sacrifice was demonstrated by Jesus himself, in his life and on the cross, His disciples, apostles and believers, called Christians, followed his example. They all gave up their lives, sacrificed them, for the gospel's sake. So what about you? These Christians, followers of Christ, might have chosen to resume their old lives after Jesus' resurrection; but they couldn't because they had received a new life, in the kingdom of God. This new life in Jesus was so precious that they were willing to die rather than give it up or deny their saviour. Are you a spectator, someone who just goes along with life? Or do you want to make a difference and receive something that's so precious, that you would die for it? The good news is that Jesus died in your place so you can receive this new and precious life now. You will have to suffer and sacrifice many things from your old life. But that is no comparison to your reward. Jesus needs you. You need Jesus, to make and show a difference in your life and others around you. Just come as you are, as I did. It's better than being a spectator. You could be a participator.

With trepidation I write about my saviour Jesus Christ. I wouldn't even be writing to you without his loving sacrifice for me. If you were the only person in the world, He would still have died for you. If your child fell into the sea, what you would do? Without thought for your own life you would dive in after them. Why? Because of love. You want to save them, because you are their father. Your father God gave you that inbuilt love from the beginning. Whether you believe in God or not, nothing has changed today. Because if your children misbehave you still love them no matter what. The difference with your heavenly father is that he loves you so much, he sent his only begotten son purposely to die for you, to save you, even though you might not know or believe in Him. He did it because it was the only way that you could be redeemed, rescued from the rudiments of this world, so that He could have a loving and personal relationship with you. God has got the same need as us. He wants to be loved and He wants to show His love. Having a loving relationship with you is God's desire, because we are His children. What father wouldn't want a loving relationship with His children. The only way you can have a full and proper relationship with God and others is through Christ and His sacrifice for you and me. You will have to read the Bible for yourself to receive a total revelation of Jesus Himself.

For now, I want to write about His life in reference to his unselfishness. Many times it is written, without apology, that only through Jesus can you come. This means you must have, in fact His totally sinless, life in you, and following His example, You must nail to the cross Your life – the temporary bit that you paint and pamper – in order to live in the spirit with Him for ever. Sin separates you from God and from others on earth. God hates sin, and it's a barrier that's got to come down in your life. But that can only be attained through following Jesus' example. So, what humble and unselfish qualities were evident in Jesus life? I tell you reader, every word He spoke was a sacrificial word for you. Yes you; not for Him. He took no reward in anything He said all His life. Can you just grasp that, reader? Everything He said was for your edification. He wouldn't even accept being called good,

> Why callest me good? There is none good but one, that is, God. (Matthew 19:17)

> Then answered Jesus and said unto them, 'Verily, verily, I say unto you. The Son can do nothing of himself, but what he seeth the Father do: for what things soever he doeth, these also doeth the Son likewise. For the Father loveth the Son, and showed him all things that himself doeth: and he will show him greater works than these, that ye may marvel'. (John 5:19–20)

God can show you also greater works in your life if you accept, as Jesus himself did, no personal reward in your benevolence. Give God the glory, because everything that is, He created – even you.

> Love not the world, neither the things that are in the world. If any man love the world, the love of the Father is not in him. For all that

is in the world, the lust of the flesh, and the lust of the eyes, and the pride of life, is not of the Father, but is of the world. And the world passeth away, and the lust thereof: but he that doeth the will of God abideth forever. (1 John 3:15–17)

I have mentioned every word of Jesus spoke was for you, but every step Jesus made was for you too. Every step was a demonstatable physical sacrifice of the flesh down the sacrificial road to Calvary, where Jesus was crucified for me and for you. I don't apologise for saying this folks; but you have got to walk the same way on that same sacrificial road – unselfishly – only doing and saying what Jesus would want you to do in every circumstance and in every step also that you take in your life.

The Son of man must suffer many things, and be rejected of the elders and chief priests and scribes, and be slain, and be raised the third day. And he said unto them all, If any man come after me, let him deny himself, and take up his cross daily, and follow me. For whosoever will save his life shall lose it: but whosoever will lose his life for my sake, the same shall save it. For what is a man advantaged, if he gains the whole world, and lose himself, or be cast away? (Luke 9:22–25)

What fantastic scripture. It says it all. Can you now read slowly, with reverence, thinking of the scene, the noise, the despair, the pain? Can you see Jesus? Can you see Him? Please, I want you to see Him struggling up Calvary road, carrying His own cross, every stripe and every step was for you; yes you, just as you are. Oh, such love. They crucified Him. He went willingly, quietly, for you and me, sinless, all because of love.

Greater love hath no man than this that a man lay down his life for his friends. (John 15:3)

> Then said Jesus, Father, forgive them; for they know not what they do. (Luke 23:34)

> And when Jesus had cried with a loud voice, he said, Father, into thy hands I commend my spirit: and having said thus, he gave up the ghost. (Luke 23:46)

You must forgive. It was the last instruction Jesus made. It's so important. He forgave them. So what about you? If you don't forgive, hell is your reward: now on earth, in your life and for ever. There is no reward in unforgiveness, only self-inflicted pain, your energy and life wasted in self pity, robbed, feeling sorry for yourself. Why not do as Jesus did? Nail self to the cross in your life and be set free from unforgiveness. Heaven is your reward now, Don't forget the instigator of your pain, the devil himself. Blame him and be set free to feel the love and warmth of your Father God demonstrated through His only begotten Son Jesus Christ. Come. Come into His arms and feel the warmth as I did. Come out of this cold, cold world. Come and sit at His table. There is a place prepared for you. Jesus says to you, reader,

> Let not your heart be troubled: ye believe in God, believe also in me. In my Father's house are many mansions: if it were not so, I would have told you. And if I go to prepare a place for you, I will come again, and receive you unto myself; that where I am, there ye may be also. (John 14:1–3)

If you want your spirit to be in the hand of God, as Jesus commended His, you must do as it says in Scripture. Deny yourself and pick up your cross daily, which is your reasonable service. Reader, if you walk the same unselfish path in life as Jesus walked every day, as you walk further and nearer your own sacrifice, nailing your own flesh to your own cross, sinless, you will then be raised from death into life, in the kingdom of God now and for ever. Amen.

The cross is the only pathway from illusion to reality. So what about you today? I've exhausted and emptied myself of words and examples of selfish and unselfish (opposites) lives, because I know that it's so important that you get this. There is no sin or self, or man's system, in heaven. They must be sacrificed to receive heaven on earth and everlasting life with your Father in heaven.

> Jesus said unto him, 'I am the way, the truth and the life: no man cometh unto the Father, but by me'. (John 14:6)

> And behold, the veil of the temple was rent in twain from the top to the bottom; and the earth did quake, and the rocks rent. (Matthew 27:51)

It's important that I explain what the Scripture above means. It happened just after Jesus had died on the cross. The veil in question belonged to the old Covenant. The Israelites, instructed by God, built a tabernacle in the desert as a place of worship to house the Ark of the Covenant and to sacrifice their best animals unto God for atonement of their sin. The veil separated the outer tabernacle from the inner part where the Ark was, in the holy place, where God would only allow the high priest to scatter blood of the sacrifice on and around the Ark, which contained the Ten Commandments written on stone. The veil represented the partition or barrier between man and God, heaven and earth, the world and the kingdom. It was symbolic of the barrier representing sin in our lives. Sin could not be permitted to enter the holy place.

> And, behold, the veil of the temple was rent in twain from the top to the bottom; and the earth did quake, and the rocks rent'. 'For Christ also hath once suffered for sins, the just for the unjust, that he might bring us to God, being put to death in the flesh, but quickened by the spirit. (Matthew 27:51)

For he hath made him to be sin for us, who knew no sin; that
we might be made the righteousness of God in him. (2 Cor. 5:21)

So we have to follow Jesus' perfect example, by tearing asunder
our veil, which is sin from our lives that keeps us out of the holy
place where we can have a relationship with our father God.
The veil that we all have is our sin, because all have sinned. By
accepting Jesus in our lives, our desire changes and then we
naturally want to eradicate sin, the veil, from our lives. How do
we do this? By sacrificing our lives daily, as the example Jesus
set, to self (flesh), sin, and the world's system, and then joyfully
seeing the veil come down, giving us a direct line to our Father.
Thank you Jesus, because you are the way, the truth, and the
life, that we must follow, even to the cross. Amen.

Salvation

The Bible is like a pair of spectacles, if you read it, it will make you see more clearly about the truth of creation and why you came to be. I personally was saved, rescued from sin and myself which I sacrificed to become nothing of myself, but Jesus all in all of my life. I had to know the old life in me to know and recognise the new life I had received in Jesus. Knowing the old life makes me appreciate and value so much my salvation and to be part of God's plan for my life. I know I was dead to life, but now alive in Jesus. That's how much of a difference it has made. Salvation gave me a reason to live life to the full. We are all made to live our lives unto God through the example of Jesus Christ. If we don't conform our lives will go wrong, and we will suffer. It's like trying to make a car do what a tractor does: it will suffer and skid around going all over the place, trying to do something it was not made to do. Eventually it will get stuck in the mire and break-down. It's never too late to start again, to start afresh as I did. You see, the things you see with your eyes are temporary and are of no effect in eternity. So don't live to them. Even you are temporary. So why live to you and not God? It's futile, pointless. The truth of creation is,

> Jesus answered and said unto him, 'Verily, verily, I say unto thee, except a man be born again, he cannot see the kingdom of God'. (John 3:3)

For God so loved the world, that he gave his only begotten son, that whosoever believeth in him should not perish, but have everlasting life. For God sent not his son into the world to condemn the world; but that the world through him might be saved. He that believeth on him is not condemned: but he that believeth not is condemned already, because he hath not believed in the name of the only begotten Son of God. (John 3:16–18).

You see, to be born again is a free gift from God. You can't earn it, but you must give up, give in, give all, repent, believe and be saved from your sin and receive a new spiritual content of righteousness and all God's virtues, in and through Jesus Christ. Jesus says you must be born again. That means changed from an old life of sin to the new life without sin. If it wasn't from one state to a different state, it could not be recognised, or valued, or precious, they are totally opposites, planned from the beginning. Or again Jesus who was in the beginning would have been of none effect and died in vain, in fact there would be no point Him even being. That is another reason why sin had to come into the world or we couldn't go from, to, because if there is only one state you are trapped, you can't go anywhere with no free will to choose, because there is no choice without an opposite.

I realize God never got anything wrong in creation. So in my life, I accept how things are, good and bad, ups and downs. If you don't accept, or take on board the truth of how it is, you can't live the life. You will always be complaining, as though you have all the answers. Life is not a competition. I don't have to compete any more, because I have accepted Jesus died for me and overcame all the doubts, the striving, the pain, the sickness, the sin, myself, the world's system, even death, because He rose again from the dead. Yes, even victory over death for you and me. So all fear of death is vanquished. Alleluia. 'And Jesus said unto them,

I am the bread of life: he that cometh to me shall never hunger; and he that believeth on me shall never thirst'. (John 6:35)

For Christ also hath once suffered for sins, the just for the unjust, that he might bring us to God, being put to death in the flesh, but quickened by the Spirit. (1 Peter 3:18)

But he was wounded for our transgressions; he was bruised for our iniquities: the chastisement of our peace was upon him; and with his stripes we are healed. (Is. 53:5)

Jesus demonstrated how we should eliminate sin in our lives on the cross He said in

And at the ninth hour Jesus cried with a loud voice, saying, 'Eloi, Eloi, Lama sabachthani?' Which is, being interpreted, My God, my God, why hast thou forsaken me? (Mark 15:34)

I have added this scripture to explain why Jesus shouted this from the cross. People used to say, God even forsook Jesus on the cross, so why shouldn't He forsake you? It's very important that you get this clear reader. If you don't already know, Jesus took all the world's sin on his back and in that sacrifice for me and you, He was separated from his father and so our sin He bore as a man and suffered, even to the separation from His Father. That's why He shouted 'God' and not 'Father'. He did it for you and me. Amen. I must tell you it doesn't mean we will stop sinning. It means Jesus showed us a *way* to stop sinning which is the only way, the truth. You must sacrifice fully your life, by nailing the worthless bit, the flesh, your selfishness, to the cross. Please follow Jesus and receive a new and fruitful life. Be born again. He wants you in heaven with Him one day. I'm sure you do too. He is waiting for you to call, 'Jesus, help me a sinner'. Again let me quote

Greater love hath no man than this that a man lay down his life for his friends. (John 15:13)

Regarding our sacrifice too,

> Hereby perceive we the love of God, because he laid down his life for us: and we ought to lay down our lives for the brethren. (1 John 3:16)

> I know that whatsoever God doeth, it shall be forever: nothing can be put to it, nor anything taken from it: and God doeth it, that men should fear before him. (Ec. 3:14) Amen.

Perfection

Jesus said, 'Be ye therefore perfect, even as your Father which is in heaven is perfect'. Matthew 5:48, and in 2 Corinthians 13:11. 'Finally, brethren, farewell. Be perfect, be of good comfort, be of one mind, live in peace; and the love of God and peace shall be with you'. Paul said in Ephesians 4:13. 'Till we come in the unity of the faith, and of the knowledge of the Son of God, unto a perfect man, unto the measure of the stature of the fullness of Christ', and in Philippians 3:15, 'Let us therefore, as many as be perfect, be thus minded: and if in anything ye be otherwise minded, God shall reveal even this unto you'. 'Whom we preach, warning everyman, and teaching everyman in all wisdom; that we may present everyman perfect in Jesus Christ'. Colossians 1:28. 'That the man of God may be perfect, thoroughly furnished unto all good works'. Timothy 3:17. 'Therefore leaving the principles of the doctrine of Christ let us go on to perfection; not laying again the foundation of repent-ance from dead works, and of faith toward God'. Hebrews 6:1. 'But let patience's have her perfect work, that ye may be perfect and entire, wanting nothing'. James 1:4. 'But the God of all grace, who hath called us unto his eternal glory by Jesus Christ, after that ye have suffered a while, make you perfect, establish, strengthen, settle you'. 1 Peter 5:10. 'And when Abraham was ninety years old and nine, the Lord appeared to Abraham, and said unto him, I am the Almighty God; walk before me, and be thou perfect'. Genesis 17:1. 'For it became him, for whom are all things, and by whom are all things, in bringing many sons unto glory, to make the captain of their salvation perfect through suffering'. Hebrews 2:10.

I don't apologize for quoting so much Scripture on perfection, even though some Christians may be heard to say 'We can't be perfect', God, Jesus, the disciples and many times, Paul speak of perfection. Are you going to argue with them? I tell you, if you have perfection within you namely, Jesus Christ, wouldn't He want to do a perfect work within you also? Of course He would: because it's God's desire and love for you. Or are you saying Christ wasn't perfect, so, you can't be perfect? God forbid! I tell you, if you say these things, Christ suffered for nothing. Or Christ is not in you? The alternative and there is only one, is to go on to imperfection, or stay imperfect. Is that what you are saying? How can you go on to imperfection? You are imperfect already. You must go on to perfection, the oppos-ite. The truth of creation is, as scripture says, your salvation made perfect through the suffering of Christ. He died that we might be made perfect. If you accept Jesus in your life, you accept to die to self. He can't get in if you are still here. We get in the way of what God wants to do in our lives through Christ. Don't forget, God sent Him. Yea God sent his son, knowingly, to die for you and me. It was the only way planned from the beginning. Believe and be saved. You can only receive the fullness of Christ, as I have explained earlier, through your own sacrifice. So this then allows Christ's spirit to fill the void in you to perfection because He is perfect, sinless and overflowing, with a direct communication with God, the spiritual overflow being uncorrupted and perfect, for you to desire and earnestly share with others. Or do you share with others imperfection? If so Jesus is not in you. If you are not sharing or desiring to share Jesus with others, you are as

Hebrews 6:1 says, still laying the foundation of repentance from dead works and faith towards God

with no overflowing. Without overflowing you have no desire to share, in fact you will have nothing to share, or the desire to share. Have you got a condition, old in association with the faith and yet still babes in understanding? The Christian life should be an advance, a growing day-by-day in the grace and knowledge of God. Don't determine your the-ology with experience, because you and we could be confused in the meaning of our experience and familiarity within the churchy mould. God is not the author of confusion or chaos, because He is not confused. Everything God says is consistent, coherent and unified. If you still allow people to hurt you, or have the fear of failing, you are still self-centered and proud. So stop beating yourself up with the things of this world. Don't get stuck in your own mire and give in and stagnate. Don't live unto the statistic, or you will become the statistic. Get your head up and live in all righteousness and truth, which is Christ. If you still have an enemy and you are glad that he has fallen into the pit, you are in the pit with him already; you can only get out of the pit through repentance and forgiveness. The devil will accuse you of sin that has already bean forgiven. Run to the cross of Jesus with your sin, not away from it because He already knows about it. There are no secrets with God. Life is in the Bible and in the relationship with God through Jesus Christ. You must have it to receive the power of His word to change lives. So follow the infallible rule of the interpretation of Scripture, it's the Scripture itself. Do you still recognize the benefits of being a Christian? I want to encourage you. Stop putting yourself down. Please digest the Scripture and stop wasting your time looking at and competing with others. Its Gods grace is sufficient for you dear reader. Please get this: you can't get to heaven just by knowing the whole Bible and quoting and memorising Scripture like some people, who make you feel inferior. You can't get to heaven with your wisdom, knowledge, riches, self-righteousness or your denomination which is of man and not God, but of division equals the devil, it's no good being a member of a denomination, but only because your name is written in the lamb's (Jesus') book of life. Get this, only through repentance and sacrifice of sin and living in all righteousness, going on to perfection, through your beloved Jesus Christ can you come, and be redeemed to your beloved father God and sit at His right hand. It's the truth. It's the life. I am going to quote this Scripture again because it's so important you get this.

> Hereby perceive we the love of God, because he laid down his life for us, and we ought to lay down our lives for the brethren. (1 John 3:16)

Jesus laid down his life for all and I mean all the world. Come on. God wants us to do the same. We can't do it for the whole world as Jesus did, but we can do it for the brethren, to carry on the work of Jesus on earth, so that people can see Jesus in us, to set that same example, not of us but of him. We are not the workman but the tool. It is not I, but Christ through me, an instrument of God. Could God say of you. 'This is my beloved son of whom I am well pleased'? If so, the world would be a better place.

Scripture says about the ultimate purpose of Christ's mission to the world:

> I in them, and thou in me, that they may be made perfect in one; and that the world may know that thou has sent me, and hast loved them, as thou hast loved me. (John 17:23)

Who could put it better than Jesus himself? Paul says in Scripture that the old life has to die for the new life to live.

> I am crucified with Christ: nevertheless I live; yet not I but Christ liveth in me: and the life which I now live in the flesh I live by the faith of the Son of God, who loved me, and gave himself for me. (Galatians 2:20)

There is nothing more I could say or add to this Scripture. It's now up to you. You could say I don't want to know about God. That's your choice; but God, through his infinite grace, love and mercy, will keep knocking on your door hoping that you will open it one day to the kingdom and a life beyond compare. Through humility, sacrifice and the spirit of God through Christ working within you, Paul says,

> What? Know ye not that your body is the temple of the Holy Ghost which is in you, which ye have of God, and ye are not your own? For ye are bought with a price: therefore glorify God in your body, and in your spirit, which are God's. (Corinthians 6:19–20)

So you are God's representative on earth; perfect and qualified to be called the temple of the living God. That being so, all God's spiritual virtues through Jesus Christ are within you and expressed in the purpose of God for your very existence and life. If you don't seek you will never find your ultimate purpose. Diligently desire to become a temple of God with an indwelling Christ directing your path into all truths. Only then can God carry out the fullness of His purpose in your life, the reason you came. Stop wasting your time running around trying to find out what your purpose in life is. It's certainly not your worldly job. It's a spiritual gift from God, and for God, for God's edification, not yours. You have to be in that spiritual place first. First you seek the Kingdom of God and all things will be given unto you, including God's gifts and purpose, within the kingdom which is not of this world. It's a spiritual gift, if you don't live in the spirit of Jesus Christ, how can you receive your spiritual gifts and spiritual purpose that God earnestly wants you to share on earth, through God's living temple. Please first seek the Kingdom of God and all your wants will be revealed and realised. Amen.

My heart goes out to people in leadership, because I have seen the pressure they have to bear and suffer. If they work in their own strength, instead of God's strength, sometimes to the point of illness, sometimes because of their desire to share God's word with others, they take too much on. Of course the picture is not the same for everyone, as in the churches described in the book of Revelation, for example. It's because there is someone, namely Jesus Christ, in me writing these very words and imploring you to listen to what the spirit of these words is saying to you personally. I don't write these words from notes, but from my heart, directly from the throne of God, through Jesus Christ, in whom we live. Come on Christians. Give up. Give in. Give all. Sacrifice and make room for the spirit of Jesus. The kingdom wants to come mightily in your life. In fact it's coming. God is shouting, 'Get out of the way', so that perfection can enter into your life.

Free will to choose

Free will is a big subject. Are you free and have you got a will? Practically and spiritually, you are tempted and choose every day: what to eat, what to do, what to watch, what to buy, what to drink and how much. Obviously there are thousands of choices that we make every day. Generally, we know what is good for us and what is right and wrong; but through ignorance, we sometimes don't know, get it wrong, usually suffer for it, learn from it and don't do it again. That's called experience. So as we get older, the statistics are on our side. Through experience of life, we make fewer mistakes – or do we carry on doing them? It's impossible for me to tell you to, do this, or to do that, because there are thousands of dos and don'ts and thousands of circumstances in people's individual lives. You would be screaming at me, 'You don't know half mate'. And, of course, They'd be right. So it's impossible for me not to generalize. Instead, I would like to pick through a few choices that we all know about, such as, wait for it . . . smoking. Were we born to smoke? No, so why do we do it knowing that it is probably killing us. People say they enjoy it and it settles their nerves. But that's a lie. It's a drug and it's their craving for it that gets their nerves on edge. So it perpetuates itself. The drug needs the drug, not you. By the way I'm not having a go at smokers personally, so calm down now and have a fag. Is that better? No. It isn't. It's not better it's worse. So you were born in this world into many diverse circumstances, with your free will to choose, I'm not bothered whether you are royalty, rich or poor. Smokers – can you say no? Go on say, No, to that little stick of leaves! If you can't, your free will to choose has gone, you are not in control, the cigarette controls you. Your free will to choose in this area of your life has gone. Good news: it's not too late to change your will and regain your freedom from the drug. Use your 'get-out-of-jail' card. Come on fight the wiles of the devil. Put the money you waste (that's all you are putting in your body – waste) back into your pocket and put it to good use instead of using it to kill yourself. Fancy you actually paying to shorten your life. Are you nuts, or insane? Don't be one of those sad, smelly people, looking old before their time. If you can't stop for yourself, do it for your kids or others around you and get back your free-will to choose. Jesus is the answer; He will give you the desire and power to regain your free will to choose righteously.

Another big subject today is eating. I must admit that I get confused sometimes, because man says this is good for you, don't eat this, eat that. Then they change their minds and say we got it wrong. Again, like smoking, we can pay to kill ourselves, or at least shorten our lives with related diseases, making the wrong choices. The most pleasurable thing in life – some might disagree – is eating and drinking. You do it at least three times a day, or when you want. You eat what you like. The variety is enormous. You look forward to it every day of your life. What more could we enjoy? It seams a bit daft but *we* generally eat too much food, while every day somewhere in the world people are starving. So, why do we make wrong choices, eating wrong foods, or too much? Why is the wrong food available? Why do we produce food we shouldn't eat? Why do they make it easy to buy? Why do they add stuff artificially to make it taste nice and look nice? Why is it so convenient? The answer, of course, is money. Again it's your free will to choose, so why can't you say no to over-eating? If this is you, I'm afraid that you have lost your free will. So the food controls you. The mirror becomes too small to fit you in the frame. Your clothes don't fit you any more. People look at you for the wrong reason. You probably say of yourself that you are happy and have a bubbly personality to hide the fact that you are so sad within yourself. Come on, be honest, nobody wants to be overweight. If they say they do, they live a lie. I implore you to get help, to regain your free will to choose. Give your life to Jesus and He will perform a miracle in your life, He will change your desires, on the inside, which affects your outside, I know because He has done it for me, whatever your need is He has the answer.

About drinking, I'm not an expert, but I believe that my own brother shortened his life through alcohol abuse. Yes, it is abuse. Why can't we say No? Why don't we listen to the doctors when they say, you are killing yourself. Again free will is gone, you actually can't say no to living a suicidal life. You can't stop killing yourself and you are not paying a hit man to do it. You are paying for it yourself. It affects all the people around you. It takes away your dignity and it can make you poor, even homeless – on the streets in fact. It's so sad for people who press this self-destruct button, because they have mums and dads and family who love them, but who have to look-on helpless. Remember, Jesus is the answer.

When I am tempted to buy something, I ask that myself. 'Can I afford it? Do I really need it?' Can I live without it? Have you got self-control in all situations? If you are honest in answering these questions, you could save a lot of money that you would otherwise waste. It's about overcoming temptation and retaining your free will to choose.

You might wonder at this point what's all this got to do with the truth of creation, yet you must agree that the truth is we are supposed to be in control of our lives. Can I ask you, reader, are you in control of every area of your life? Like some of the examples above, have a deep think about it before you answer. The ultimate answer again is about sacrificing yourself, as Jesus did for you, that you might follow. Through sacrifice the devil (the tempter) can't make you turn to drink, or eat too much, or lose your temper, or buy things you don't need etc. I know I've mentioned it many times in the book, but it's the same issue, namely dying to self. The devil can't tempt a dead person to live to his lies and deceit and neither can you live to your selfish self, killing yourself with junk. It's the only way, to stop eating too much and the rest, it's a self thing. The world's system doesn't care one bit about you. They only want your money: you pay to eat too much and then you have to pay again to help you slim. Have you noticed how nice people can be when you are spending money with them, and then when they have got it, they change and don't want to know you? Some people are not really nice. The system trains them to be artificially nice to get your money, or any other thing they might want from you; so they are not nice. It's false, a lie. The whole service and retail system is programmed that way, people are taught to smile and be polite artificially, to get you to come back and spend more. Wouldn't it be nice if everyone was genuinely nice? Some are but it's a minority today. The devil controls this world's system and he is screwing the lid down tighter throughout society. Pressure, pressure, pressure: at home and at work. I tell you, the psychiatrists are very busy these days with more referrals than ever before. You will hurt if you are still of this world's system. So put your life in the hands of Jesus, as I did. He has all the answers. Allow Him to release the pressure in your life. Choose wisely. Stop going along with this greedy world's system, where they put money before people. Jesus is waiting for you to call-out, 'Jesus help me a sinner'.

Life

I keep to the law of the world's system, but I don't let it control me, because I have accepted that Jesus Christ died for me on the cross for my sins in the world's system, and I am forgiven. I am now stood on solid ground in the kingdom of God, not of this world, purchased with a price, loved and precious. Reader, do you feel loved and precious? Or do you feel unloved, lonely, taken for granted, used and abused, and that life's a drag, it's all repetition, meaningless, purposeless?

Jesus has all the answers to life's problems, because He says that life should not be a problem, if you would only follow His example. From the beginning of time God had a plan for you, because He loves you, and He knew you would have problems – that is why He came – Jesus has all the remedies to the ills of all mankind. Man hasn't got the answer; the problem is *with* man, so man can never disquiet the ills and despair of his kind, but Jesus can. So look to Him as I did.

> Come unto me, all ye that labour and are heavy laden and I will give you rest. (Matthew 11:28)

> And the spirit and the bride say, 'Come'. And let him that heareth say, Come. And let him that is athirst come. And whosoever will, let him take the water of life freely. (Revelation 22:17)

Jesus is constantly calling to you, so just come. You might say, 'I can't come. Just look at me; I've done so many things wrong'. Yet, that's exactly why you should come just as you are!

Repent and be forgiven. Please come to Jesus and He will give you rest and peace beyond reason. You can be forgiven and redeemed to a life with purpose, meaning and joy that will transcend even the difficult circumstances that life throws at you sometimes. Jesus will be there for you, so please come. Can you imagine if everyone lived like we should, like Jesus, sacrificially serving one another, there would be no need for police, army, locks or security, no stress, no competition, no inspection, no fear, no prisons, no pressure, no hatred, no despair, no pride, no starving, no drugs, no homelessness, no want, no evil, no jealousy, no divorce, no lies and deceit, no greed, no debt, no vanity, no discontent, no defilement, no earnestness, no neglect, no envy, no depression, no unfaithfulness, no friendlessness, no waste, no judgment, no sadness, no ingratitude, no offences, no opposers, no dishonour, no sorrow, no injustice, no covetousness, no death, no retaliation, no anger, no disobedience, no impatience, no poverty, no adversity, no falseness, no unrest, no denominations, no unrighteousness, no religiosity, no wickedness, no condemnation, no selfishness, no sin, no pitilessness, no strife, no falsehood, no immorality, no unworthiness, no worldliness, no abuse and no guilt . . . Unfortunately in the truth of creation, the opposites of these things had to be, so that we could recognise and assign to the qualities that Jesus brings. The entire list above is just to make you stop and think what a world it could be. You come and you go. But where are you now? Where you are now is where you are going. Your past doesn't need to dictate your future, so stop blaming God, since He has given you a free will, a chance to change from self, sin and the world's system, through Jesus Christ. Don't wait for the world to change so that everything will be allright. The world is on a downward spiral that cannot be reversed, and it will take you with it if you don't resist it in your life. Sin is lawlessness of the human will, a rebellion against God, which deprives it of fellowship with God. It is a living death, where hell will be your reward. Jesus doesn't want that for you, so please don't waste His sacrifice. He grieved and denied Himself for you. If you don't submit to what God says in your life, the good will never come to pass, so both are robbed of the reward, of eternal life and of your citizenship in heaven. Why settle for less in your life? Step out of the ordinary into the extraordinary way of life. Why live to this world when you are going to leave it eventually, whatever happens? Leave it now. Step into the kingdom, Jesus has paid the price for your sin, so just believe and you will be saved.

> For what is a man profited, if he shall gain the whole world, and lose his own soul? Or what shall man give in exchange for his soul? (Matthew 16:26)

> Set your affection on things above, not on things of the earth. (Colossians 3:2)

> Teaching us that, denying ungodliness and worldly lusts, we should live soberly, righteously, and Godly, in this present world. (Titus 2:12)

Let's think about the progress on someone's life. Here's an example. It's called, 'I'm getting older'. Where are we now? We are making choices, worldly choices or Godly choices. Are they selfish or unselfish decisions and what is my future in my repetitive life?

I'm born – I'm getting older . . .
I'm going to school, I'm getting older . . .
Taken exams, I'm getting older . . .
Been on holiday, I'm getting older . . .
Taking driving lessons, I'm getting older . . .
I go out clubbing, I'm getting older . . .
Took my driving test, I'm getting older . . .
I'm going to college, I'm getting older . . .

Got a degree, I'm getting older . . .
I got a job, I'm getting older . . .
I'm buying a house, I'm getting older . . .
I'm getting married, I'm getting older . . .
We got a dog, I'm getting older . . .
I passed my driving test, I'm getting older . . .
We go to the pub, I'm getting older . . .
We go to church, I'm getting older . . .
We have some kids, I'm getting older . . .
I'm making a lot of money, I'm getting older . . .
I've bought a place abroad, I'm getting older . . .
I've bought a small boat, I'm getting older . . .
We have put a conservatory on our house, I'm getting
older . . .
My kids are going to school, I'm getting older . . .
They are at university, I'm getting older . . .
The kids are costing me a fortune, I'm getting older . . .
I've seen a lot of the world, I'm getting older . . .
I am overweight, I'm getting older . . .
I now go to the gym, I'm getting older . . .
I go to the cinema, I'm getting older . . .
I've not much money now, I'm getting older . . .
We have just moved house, I'm getting older . . .
My kids have got married, I'm getting older . . .
Now I'm a grandad, I'm getting older . . .
I've been ill lately, I'm getting older . . .
Regular hospital visits, I'm getting older . . .
We have paid our mortgage off, I'm getting older . . .
We have worked hard all our lives you know, I'm getting
older . . .
Retirement, I'm getting older . . .
We have achieved a lot, I'm getting older . . .
I've made a lot of mistakes, I'm getting older . . .
I do a lot of walking, I'm getting older . . .

I'm trying not to put on weight, I'm getting older . . .

I like to reminisce, I'm getting older . . .

I baby sit now, I'm getting older . . .

My ears and eyes are not the same, I'm getting older . . .

My kids are telling me what to do, I'm getting older . . .

I spoil my grandkids, I'm getting older . . .

My grandkids are always at our house, I'm getting older . . .

I go on bus trips, I'm getting older . . .

I'm a lot quieter now, I'm getting older . . .

I thought I had a future, I'm getting older . . .

Checking my will, I'm getting older . . .

Shall I be burned or buried?, I'm getting older . . .

The old folks home? Never, I'm getting older . . .

Oh go on then, I'm getting older . . .

I've been going to a lot of funerals lately, I'm getting older . . .

What have I contributed to mankind and this world? I'm getting older . . .

Who have I helped, I'm getting older . . .

Wish I hadn't smoked, I'm getting older . . .

Those motorized chairs are ok, I'm getting older . . .

Those beds that move are good too, I'm getting older . . .

I wish I had . . ., I'm getting older . . .

I wish I hadn't . . ., I'm getting older . . .

Television is getting on my nerves, I'm getting older . . .

Life seems pointless, I'm getting older . . .

I love my kids and grandkids, I'm getting older . . .

I'm very critical nowadays, I'm getting older . . .

I'm suffering a lot, I'm getting older . . .

Life's just an exercise about dying, I'm getting older . . .

I don't go out now, I'm getting older . . .

I'm just waiting to go, I'm old. Haven't I been lucky to get old, the alternative is to die young, so it's good to get old.

Just sit back and think for a while, you are young: looking forward, middle-aged: looking both ways, and old:

looking back at your life. A Christian life is always positive, looking forward and is not dependant on age. Reader, do you think life as outlined above is that practical? What would be the point of just coming and going, with a bit in the middle and your offspring doing the same down the generations? I tell you I know a God who has a destiny and purpose for every human being on earth. It is a destiny which was set in place before anything was, the end before the beginning. God made everything to exist for a reason, nothing and no-one is by accident, not even you. If you don't know the maker you will never know your purpose and destiny for life. You could sabotage your destiny by your wrong decisions. So protect your purpose and safeguard your destiny by living unto the example that Jesus set. Choose wisely. God can even take all the bad things and turn them round for good, not just because He is obliging; but because it is in His interest. If you are in the right place in creation and carrying out His purpose, representing Him and glorifying Him in your life, setting a good example that others might follow, that is God's plan for everybody on earth, so it is your eternal destiny. God never changes your purpose in life or your destiny. It's fixed, and it's only your decisions that are not fixed which can change it. So call on your maker, through Jesus Christ, that you might find yourself and regain purpose in life and so secure your destiny in the right place which is heaven on earth.

Our Thoughts

Let's put size and significance into life, a scientist on the television says that there are probably one hundred billion stars in our galaxy, and probably one hundred billion galaxies. That's too big for man to even contemplate. Does it end, or is it a circle? If it is a circle, what's outside the circle? Will we never know? To you and me vast though they are, the statistics don't make one jot of difference to our lives, but I think it's good to think on these things and compare these to our human form which is so small in comparison, but just as complex, made-up of things that we cannot see with our naked eye. Although our bodies don't change, (apart from ageing) there is one thing that does change and that makes us different. This is our mind. The mind can think right and wrong, it can think negative or positive, it can have a spir-itual argument with in itself it can control our emotions, it controls our imagination, thoughts about sex good or evil. We can change our minds in a split second. In fact our mind makes hundreds of decisions every day: what to eat, about work, driving, holidays and so on. Within your mind analysis takes place on the right and the left. So purify your mind and then you will win the argument.

> And be not conformed to this world: but be transformed by the renewing of your mind, that ye may prove what is that good, and acceptable, and perfect, will of God. (Romans 12:2)

In all this vastness and with billions of people on this earth, you may feel insignificant, worthless, but whosoever you are I can tell you, that you are very precious and loved by your father God. What human father wouldn't love his child? So make your thoughts wise and good ones,

> Finally, brethren, whatsoever things are true, whatsoever things are honest, whatsoever things are just, whatsoever things are pure, whatsoever things are lovely, whatsoever things are of good report; if there be any virtue, and if there be any praise, think of these things. (Philippians 4:8)

> Let this mind be in you, which was also in Christ Jesus. (Philippians 2:5)

It would be good for everybody to write about their lives, in fact to keep a diary of events, they would be so diverse. There is one man I have met and put my arms round, who fits this criteria, his name is General Charles Duke, an astronaut, who has stood on the moon. I suppose that If you argue with him what you want out of life, his reply would probably be, give your life to Jesus, standing on the moon has no comparison to the love of God, through Jesus Christ, live and do everything unto Jesus, only then does your life become worthwhile, even standing on the moon.

Judgment

Imagine there was a disc being made about everything in your life. Every word you've said or thought every person you have met are going to be recorded on it for Jesus to see. In fact your whole life is laid out at His feet. Whether you believe in God or not, one day you will be judged by Jesus.

> The Lord knoweth how to deliver the godly out of temptation, and to reserve the unjust unto the Day of Judgment to be punished. (2 Peter 2:9)

How do you feel about this? Embarrassed? Ashamed? Guilty? Would you want to do a runner? or would you wish you had another chance? Since you are reading this book now, you do have another chance, even if you haven't read the Bible. Let me tell you, you have a chance to be forgiven, to have the slate wiped clean. But if you don't take it the verdict on your life will be that you are guilty as charged. Hell fire and torment will be your destiny. I tell you, reader, hell is a real place. So what are you going to do about it?

Now is your opportunity to cry out 'Stop the disc. I want to start again!' And to pray this prayer: 'Please forgive me Lord a sinner, I'm sorry for what I have done, I accept that you died for me on the cross for my sins, and were raised from the dead. Lord you stopped and started time, so please stop my disc and give me a new one, so I can start again. Thank you Jesus'.

We all have to come one way through Jesus Christ, yes I came and I can honestly say that I too wouldn't want my old disc of my life to be played. Don't forget living is giving for the right reason.

I, even I, am he that blotteth out thy transgressions for mine own sake, and will not remember thy sins. (Isaiah 43:25)

Service

Wherefore we are receiving a kingdom which cannot be moved, let us have grace, whereby we may serve God acceptably with reverence and Godly fear. (Hebrews 12:28)

A servant's duty is to obey his master. Jesus himself washed the disciples' feet, demonstrating to them that they were chosen to serve, just like Him a servant of God. You were bought with a price at the cross. You are not your own. So are you obeying your master in serving the kingdom of God's serving others, as though everyone you serve is Jesus himself? That's the level of service God requires of you to carry out His perfect will and His purpose in your very life.

I tell you the truth, if someone had said twenty years ago, that I would be a Christian, and that I would be writing a book on the subject, I obviously wouldn't have believed them. But I know it's true and I know God has used people mightily through the centuries, but I didn't think anything so profound would happen to me, especially in an area that I am weak in. So I want to encourage you, you must allow God to prepare you to carry out His perfect plan for your life, He certainly hasn't chosen you for nothing. So get walking faster down the sacrificial road of your life, where God will give you all His attributes and equip you for His will and purpose in your very life, as He has for me.

And we know all things work together for good to them that love God, to them who are called according to his purpose. (Romans 8:28)

But so shall it not be among you: but whosoever will be great among you, shall be your minister. And whosoever of you will be the chiefest, shall be servant of all. (Mark 10:43–44)

Heaven and Hell

In the truth of creation without the opposite we wouldn't have heaven or hell, planned from the beginning, stemmed from the knowledge of the tree of good and evil in the Garden of Eden. Which one are you choosing in your life? There would be no point having one without the other, we would have a free for all if only one state existed. For example, if there was only hell, there would be no point being good. The same applies if there was only heaven, again there would be no point being good, if we were all going to the same place. So obviously in the truth of creation, God created and planned heaven and hell in the beginning, because there would be no point in creation, no difference, no choice, no standards, no fear, no reward and no redemption into heaven, it would be impossible for either state to exist without the other. The whole world is cursed in sin. Jesus' plan from the beginning, was to be made a curse for us on the cross – yes, He came to die for us – that we might follow Him, giving us a chance to live a heavenly life on earth, going on into eternity, all because of *love*, such *love*. To let you know how much the Father loves you. He gave his only begotten Son for you. Follow and your eternal reward is to be with someone who would give His life for you and to be in heaven together forever. Reader do you know any one on earth who loves you that much? You have done nothing for Jesus, but He is still willing to give so much. His very life, for the whosoever. He loves you that much that He sent His Holy Spirit, His comforter in person to guide you to Him. Being born again into Jesus is like an engagement to be married and your intended is Jesus, waiting for you and beckoning you with open arms to come to the wedding. Please come, face-to-face with Jesus in heaven, the love of your eternal life. Jesus said

> As the Father has loved me, so have I loved you: continue ye in my love. (John 15:9)

The alternative or opposite to heaven, hell, is not worth thinking about. Look around the world, look what's happened in the past and look what's happening now. If you think hell doesn't exist, consider how some people live their lives. consider the unnecessary conflict between God's people, with no forgiveness. I know that it is not easy to forgive when innocent people are dying, but it is God's way. The alternative is to carry on hating and killing, which just escalates, it doesn't do any good or solve anything, fighting over land and the things of this world that we will never own. I'm not saying that we shouldn't protect ourselves personally, or nationally. The devil throws the spanner in, using people to commit horrendous crimes of hate against humanity. How do we respond? We pick up the spanner ourselves and start dismantling and killing innocent people ourselves to save face and it is still going on. The devil just loves it. He's got us all at it. What do the perpet-rators achieve? Loss of innocent lives and anarchy. What was the response? What the attackers expected and wanted: retaliation. Was anything really achieved? No, apart from opening more hornets' nests of hate between God's people, so more innocent lives being lost. Why not do it God's way and forgive. I know it's not easy, but the devil hates forgiveness. There is much more to be gained in the power of forgiveness, which can bring victory over the powers of darkness, and dignity to mankind. Jesus came to destroy the works of the devil. Through His own temptation and forgiveness He set an example that we might follow. I pray that followers of Jesus who are in government and in places of authority, will start to make the right decisions that affect us all. They need to do what Jesus would do in every situation or circumstance. And it's the same for you, dear reader in all the decisions, even minor ones that you make, ask yourself what Jesus would do. I tell you He has all the answers. Amen.

Man, for all manner of reasons, wants to hurt, hate and even kill our fellow man, because of history. The new generation doesn't have to keep hating; because they played no part in it, they weren't even born, so why hate because of history. There is no resolution in killing our fellow man, it just makes it worse, I implore young people of this generation, to stand up and say stop to this madness. Let's have reconsideration, forgiveness and understanding for each other and then maybe the past can be accepted as past, creating a platform where young people of the world, can help and even love one another, no matter what the past says, because it's not their past, so why should you young people suffer in other peoples past mistakes. Young people of the world stand up together and say enough is enough; we are not going to live your life. You don't have to come together with your religion, color or creed, just come together because you are the same, with respect for who you are, human beings.

MY PERSONAL TESTIMONY

I feel it will help to know a little of my life now that you have read *The Truth of Creation*.

I tell you the truth, God gave me wealth that I always lusted after, a lovely devoted wife and two beautiful daughters. Like most people I thought I'd got what I'd always wanted, so I should now be totally happy because I'd achieved the worldly criteria for happiness, But within myself I was still not satisfied, nor did I have or peace of mind until. I was born again at 7:30 am on the 25th of February 1989, aged 43 years old.

My life totally changed, not just my life but everything, yes everything, From that date I knew the answer to life for all mankind was Jesus Christ.

How we started in business

My wife had worked in a garden and Interflora shop from leaving school. She had worked hard for the owners, after managing the business for them in their obsence. Sadly the owner was dying of leukemia but before he died he asked us to go to the local pub for a drink, to be polite I went. We then went back to his home for a coffee, but unknown to us he had planned for the accountant to be there to talk me into buying his business – something which I had declined earlier. Anyway, they talked me into buying it there and then, making sure the price was what I could afford to pay, because my wife's employer wanted her to have the business. I myself didn't want the business at that time because I was working as an electrician, which I enjoyed. I just didn't fancy working in one place selling flowers and the like, but we took it on anyway.

The transition was a new and big learning curve for me, but I soon settled down and got on with it, learning mainly from the customers. After eleven years new garden centres were springing up and I couldn't compete with them on price, so I found some land – it was an old garage and compound – with the idea of starting my own garden centre. I phoned the agents for the asking price which was sixty nine thousand pounds, but all I had was the value of my house. So I cheekily offered them thirty five thousand which they declined, to put it mildly. A couple of weeks later the agents rang and said pay up in ten days and you can have the land for thirty five thousand pounds – my offer. So I went to the bank and got a bridging loan and purchased the land for virtually half price. We eventually sold our house for thirty thousand pounds, because we needed the money fast. My wife was apprehensive, even in tears at the thought of leaving our (then) new home with the girls aged six and eight years old, and moving to a caravan on our new land. I was so positive and enthusiastic that I said I would build us a new five bedroomed bungalow on the site. To her credit, there's one thing I can say and that is my wife always believed in me; if I said I would do something I always did. I still don't know how we managed, because my wife was still running the old business on her own with the children in tow and I was trying to open the existing garage into a small shop. To top it all there was a miner's strike which lasted a full year, although we helped the miners out, they still smashed our windows, and the like. So the development of the business was put on hold, because of lack of customers and funds and our stay in the caravan was prolonged to two and a half years. You may think it was rough, but to be honest we were very happy and cosy with the children in the caravan. I worked day and night on the bungalow and eventually we moved in. It was very exciting for us all, because it had taken so long. I remember the kids used to sleep on the floor in our bedroom, because they were frightened of all the space that they weren't used to, but we all settled down eventually.

I installed a very large glass house attached to the old garage and then the business started to pick up giving us enough funds to sell the old business. Looking back I don't know how my wife ran the old business for five years on her own with two young children, but at last we were able to work together again. As the business increased we built on and on and then we made a mistake: we bought another garden centre. The pressure, organising staff and everything was crazy. My brother in law managed the new business, which we eventually sold to him at a loss, because we were getting so much busier. We were also getting older, and that created an imbalance in our lives that we couldn't sustain. On the old pit tip and old railway lines adjacent to us; they built a forty acre lake and a golf course, which increased our business dramatically.

God was in our lives, before we knew him. He knew us and had His mighty hand upon us, guarding and guiding us in all that we did. There is no other explanation, for your glory we live, thank you Jesus. My wife and I seemed to have been working seven days a week for about thirty years. We had the usual ups and downs in our lives, but my priority in my life was making money. At forty years old I said to my wife, I don't know what's happening to me but I'm starting to see things differently: nature and the like. That certainly was not the norm for me, because I was too busy making money to think of such things. I also said that forty was a good age to be, as I could look back over all my mistakes, learn from them and put them right. I thought if I did that I probably would have more peace and maybe start to sleep better. Our lives at that time were so busy we hardly had time to eat and bring up two young children, there was never enough time.

I did not know at the time but my youngest sister and her local church were praying for me. Not only that, a Christian salesman used to visit me every two weeks. This man always talked about Jesus and gave me little books which I never read; I just didn't want to know about Jesus because again I said I was too busy. The things this salesman said, I tried to argue against at the time, but after work what he had said kept mulling around in my mind. I couldn't believe that I never won one of those arguments; it started to make me think more deeply of what he had said. My sister asked me to go to a Christian concert in Sheffield, I said no at first. But after some pressure I agreed to go. After the concert which was quite pleasant, a man who was the pastor of the local church spoke to me and said, 'Are we going to see more of you'? In other words, are you coming to church? As an excuse I said, 'No I'm going to put my life in order first'. He then took my hand, looked me in the eye and said, 'Give your life to Jesus and he will put your life in order'. I now understand that in those three years from forty to forty three years old God was preparing my heart. I always said if there was a God he would have to get me by the scruff of the neck, as they say, and that's exactly what He did.

My Conversion

I had never believed in God or been to church but miraculously on the 25 February 1989 at 7:30 AM I woke up crying. I got on my knees, took hold of my wife on the bed and shook her, she thought I was having a bad dream. I said urgently, 'Jesus loves me and He loves you too'. From that moment time stopped for me and then re-started. But, I became a stranger, not only to my wife, but to myself too. I was in a daze that morning, I didn't know me any more. I thought I'd gone crazy, it is hard for me to explain to the reader, but basically I was doing things right, but getting things wrong also. I knew I was born again, but I really didn't know at this time what that meant, because you can't give born again any value till you are born again, if that makes any sense. It's like you don't know that you are lost, before you are found.

We went to work in my garden centre as usual like robots, because that's what our lives had become, that very same morning that I was saved, a close friend came to see me and said I've got the tickets for the mud-wrestling match. Immediately without thought, I told him I was sorry but I couldn't go. I then tried to explain the circumstances of what happened to me, that I wasn't the same any more. He just laughed and thought I was joking. Then, when he realised that I was serious, he marched off in a huff. I just couldn't go to the mud-wrestling. Something inside me just would not let me go. There was no compromise from just two hours after I had been saved. Thank you Jesus.

That evening after work I started throwing things out of the house: tapes, records, my wife's cosmetics . . . anything that wasn't natural or needed, or so I thought. My wife, bless her, just shook her head in disbelief at what I was doing. She thought I'd lost it. There was such turmoil. It was mad. The next day was Sunday. So I went to the local church; the pastor was the man I had met earlier at the concert. Before the meeting I briefly told him what had happened the morning before. The meeting, which was my first, was brilliant. I seemed to understand everything he was saying. I was amazed. It was life, but in another dimension I'd never heard before. At the end of the meeting the pastor made an altar call for anyone who wanted to accept Jesus into their lives. I immediately went forward with another man. The pastor explained to the congregation that I was already saved the morning before, but it was good to come forward publicly. I was so bubbling over inside I asked the pastor if I could address the congregation and he said come up. It blesses me now looking back to what I actually said, because I'd never read Scripture, or been to church before. Have you got the scene folks, I was beaming like a Cheshire cat and I just blurted out, 'I thought I'd got everything, but I realise now that I hadn't. But now I've got everything , I've got Jesus'. I also said, 'Jesus is at the side of me right now and he's saying if I fall he will carry me'. I stood down from the pulpit and then I asked to go up again. The pastor said, okay. I went on to say that God had said to me that I would have my own church and pulpit, the pulpit was my new till section at the garden centre and while the builders were working on the extension I would ask them to put two crosses in another coloured brick on the gable ends. The congregation was so blessed at these words there was an uproar praising God and the like. To be honest I've got tears now writing it – such good memories – I didn't realize at the time that the meeting was taped.

It was all too hard to take in at the time because there was so much happening, I soon realized that there was a lot to learn in my new life and there was no going back. I never had a desire to be a Christian. People assume that there must have been some major thing wrong in my life. On the surface there wasn't; everything was well in the business. We were, I thought quite happy. But as a Christian I realized that there were a lot of things covered up and not dealt with in our lives. People ask me if I'm one of those born again' Christians and, I say I didn't choose to be anything, let alone a Christian; but I am one because God chose me, and I'm glad He did.

A man in our assembly purchased a new King James Bible from America for me. I'd never read any book at this point, because I simply didn't have time. As soon as I started to read the Bible I was absolutely gobsmacked, as they say in Yorkshire. I just couldn't believe what I was reading. To me it was life itself, but a different life to what I had before. Of course I got it all wrong, I just couldn't put it down. Instead of running my business as usual, I would just sit in the corner and read the Bible all day. I wouldn't listen to my wife's genuine complaints. In fact I wasn't interested in anything to do with the business. The staff were doing what they wanted. The business was suffering and my wife was trying to cope on her own, bless her. I was so bold and on fire that everyone got Jesus whether they wanted it or not. Christians used to come into the centre. And nosily I would ask if they were born again. Some used to get annoyed, but I didn't care. I started telling people, including my wife and children boldly how to live their lives. They all thought I'd gone mad; the mental institution was the next step, they thought. I got so much opposition from customers family and friends that my life was in total disarray. It was just mad, but I stood my ground. No-one could understand or accept the change in me. They used to say I would soon get over it. Then a thought came to me, that I now know came from God It was, put your house in order. Wow. It was a 'wow', because I had got one major thing wrong: I was telling people how to live their lives, instead of what Jesus taught to set a good example that others might follow. I just said 'oh no' and put my hand over my mouth. If you think you are a boss, no matter what position you are in you are not part of the body of Christ. I had to learn that all are equal members. That was my first big lesson and I realised there was many more to come.

Even in my business God wanted excellence. He wanted me, not to lord it over my staff but to treat them as equals, showing them respect. Our marriage took a dive: my wife just couldn't understand me any more and we started to have many arguments because she was working even harder while I was witnessing to customers. Even when she asked me to help when we were busy, I just shrugged and carried on witnessing. One day I stood in the bedroom and shouted, while banging on the Bible, 'We live by the word of God and nothing else'; That night we ended up in separate beds. Looking back I can see how my wife must have been in so much turmoil and unhappiness. Come to think about it, I was unhappy too. It was a crazy time in our lives. I was like a bull in a china shop, nuts for Jesus, but with no control. I don't know how the pastor put up with me, bless him. Because of the turmoil I was starting to doubt whether I was now a better person, so I asked the children if they wanted their old dad back, knowing they would tell me the absolute truth. They said I was a much better dad as a Christian. As I grew in grace life started to get a little easy. I sort of started to relax a little in the Lord, in fact I actually started to sleep at night for the first time. Such a peace came over me that I stopped taking the business problems to bed. It was great.

As a family we started to attend the local church. Then one day, to my amazement, an altar call was made and my wife got up and walked to the front and gave herself to the Lord. A few months later, separately, my children also gave themselves to the Lord and soon after that we were all baptized in water together. Alleluia. That made life much easier! Everything changed. My wife now wanted to work hard so that we would have more opportunities to witness. It was now team work and we were a lot happier together as Christians, going in the same direction. I started to grow in knowledge and wisdom and while standing at the till section I called my pulpit in my garden centre I naturally started to witness to many customers and salesmen, some of the regulars couldn't believe it was me. God taught me to put customers before their money and to be totally honest with them, even telling them not to buy an item if I thought they didn't need it. I wouldn't allow customers to be rude to me and take it, as in the old days for the sake of the money, and many times I had to show them the door because my standards were now God's standards. Often, came back and apologized for what they had said. I gave everything up for God to run my garden centre His way, I knew that with Him it was in better hands than in mine, so in the first year as a Christian-run business, putting people before money, the customers trusted and respected me so much more for my honesty and integrity, that my turnover went up by a staggering two hundred thousand pounds, that same year. It was no coincidence, I'm sure.

We went on holiday to Hawaii that same year that I was saved and of course I took my Bible with me. Looking back I realised I got it all wrong again, because I read the Bible on the plane, in the hotel and on Wykeke Beach, with a towel over my head. I even sat and watched and videoed all the Christian programmes on the American television. I realise now, I had got the balance on that holiday all wrong ('Sorry, girls'). I must have been an absolute pain in the neck. One plus for me on the holiday, and a surprise, was a Christian meeting on the beach. It was fantastic, I videoed it and cried through most of the meeting, with thankfulness of course.

I attended a Christian assembly regularly but in the first year I used to cry so much it hurt. I know I had so much of my past to cry about, not self-pity, but looking back, I know

God wanted all my past revealed and brought to the surface, confessed and forgiven by God, so that I could move on in my new life as a Christian. In my experience if you don't deal with the hurts of the past and the regrets and such like those memories can keep preying into your mind. Then they affect your thoughts and feelings so you get moody and depressed. I used to do this a lot, but to stop it controlling me I had to resolve that Jesus is the answer, put the past in the bin, hold my head up and say not guilty. We have to forgive those who have hurt us, and ourselves and receive Jesus fully into our lives. He will then restore and give us an overwhelming joy and peace, no matter what the world throws at us.

It was hard for me to believe that, through Jesus, God had put his hand on me, I certainly felt that I didn't deserve it. I never used to cry, but now I had forty three years of the old life to cry about. How could I have got life so wrong? my gratitude was (and is) overwhelming. God gave me another chance, through Jesus Christ. Alleluia.

Then God started to deal with the major things of my past, one of which I had tucked away in my memory and tried not to think about it. I will never forget the day, I was having a bath and my wife was sat on the floor beside me, we were just talking. I just blurted it out that I had been sexually abused not only by a married man across the road, but also by a young women next door. The revelation of this truth to my wife I believe answered a lot of questions in our past relationship, particular when we were young. Looking back at my life I realized that I was robbed of my innocence, my personality had changed. My whole life was affected things I should have been thinking about as a child, fun and games, lightheartedness, mischief, etc. had been taken from me. Everything became serious, devious, and sordid, in fact my whole thought-pattern, towards adults in particular, was changed. I saw them differently and I certainly didn't trust them. I used to look under the bed several times a night thinking there was someone there. I also had a repeated dream that someone was chasing me. I was a very frightened child, I think I was about eight years old when I was abused and I didn't tell anyone about it until I told my wife, thirty eight years later. I know I wouldn't have told anyone if I hadn't become a Christian. I would have taken the secret to the grave. Thank you Jesus for setting me free. Alleluia. Jesus loving voice spoke to me, in my darkness. I heard it. I responded, and He was there waiting for me, I asked Him how long he had been waiting for me to confess my past. He said, 'From the beginning'. He is waiting for you too, beloved, to feel His warmth and reassurance. He is your safety net. If you fall He will catch you, you don't have to be afraid any more. His arms are out wide waiting to wrap them round His hurting little children, please come and be set free from your past. You may think nobody cares and nobody knows. But I tell you Jesus cares and knows you already. You may feel ashamed, afraid and lonely; so just allow Jesus to love you. When He calls, do respond. He will restore you, so you can help people in the same circumstances as you. Ask Him, 'Jesus please come into my life and take control and set me free to forgive; not just for a moment, but for ever'. Jesus set me free without guilt to tell anyone, so the first person I told after that was my mum, because even at this late stage in her life, I wanted her to understand why I was a problem child and that my bad behaviour wasn't her fault. She was shocked to put it mildly. It was lucky for them that the perpetrators had died young, because they were so-called friends of my mum's at the time and she wanted to give them a peace of her mind. 'Why didn't you tell me?' my mum asked. For a child's usual reasons of course: there's the guilt, the threats, the fear, the 'They wouldn't believe you', 'It's our secret', 'You know what will happen if you tell' and so on, so you keep quiet. As I got older I thought I was normal, but looking back I now know the abuse affected my whole life, I was robbed of normality. In my teenage years I was nervous, I couldn't sleep, I was very aggressive and moody, yet still frightened when I was on my own. In fact I never liked being on my own. I had total confusion about my sexuality, I thought lust was normal. I thought everyone was the same as me, but looking back from my new Christian life, I realize that I certainly was not normal. You could say sexual lust was the centre of my thought life; it occupied my mind all the time. To live as a Christian I realised that all (and I mean all) my past had to be dealt with. I had to forgive others, and also accept forgiveness for myself. It wasn't easy to accept it for myself, and without Jesus I knew I couldn't have done it.

> Then said Jesus, 'Father forgive them; for they know not what they do'. (Luke 23:34)

So if I am a follower of Jesus, who am I not to forgive also. I realized the perpetrator is the devil himself, who I blame for what happened in my young life and probably in the abuser' lives also. They were probably abused themselves. This helped me to forgive them. Don't get me wrong it's an evil act, and wants exposing. That evil contaminated my young innocent life, the memory which the memory of will stay with me all my life, but I don't use it as an excuse for my behaviour now, as some might. There are millions abused in the world, if you are one of them, my heart goes out to you. Come to Jesus as I did and He will set you free to forgive and to compassionately help others in the same situation.

> For if ye forgive men their trespasses, your heavenly Father will also forgive you. (Matthew 6:14)

I used to run away from people who hurt me, but not any more. I don't have to defend myself now. My life is not for my sake but for the gospel's sake. Instead of serving myself, I now serve the

Lord. I was saved – this means saved from self and sin. In reality I am in the world, but not of the world's system, in which I used to suffer. I am now redeemed and saved from the world into God's kingdom, which is not of this world, to do the will of God through Jesus Christ, who has given me a real purpose to live, not to just exist for a while and then die, but to live an extraordinary and eternal heavenly life now.

New Experiences

As I stood at my cash point each day, there was chaos all around me, which is the norm in a busy business; but now as a Christian I had an unbelievable peace – all the stress had gone. I was working hard in it, but I was not of it. It's hard to explain, I was not the boss any more, with all the pressures and responsibility. God took all that from me. I realized He was my new boss; everything I did was now done unto Him, and not my selfish self. It was a realization that I didn't own anything any more. I gave up. I gave in and gave all. I wasn't even my own any more. What is the point living for temporary things, even myself? My hope now is to follow and to sacrifice my life as Jesus did for others, for a greater reward than this world can offer which is death, but an eternal life with God our father in heaven.

Many people came to see me at work, to congratulate and encourage me in my new faith; but many more were critical and looking for trouble trying to trip me up, thinking because I was a Christian, I would be a pushover. But God in me was no pushover. One man came to see me privately and said I was sinning and said he wanted to pray for me. I asked him in what area I was sinning. He said covertessness. I said to him I think you are mistaken. Just because I have all this stock to sell, it's not personal, it's just business. I used say to some Christians come and stand at this side of the counter and see if you can still be like Jesus, keeping your peace, with love, forgiveness and understanding, with the world on the other side of the counter, shouting abuse, being arrogant, lying, stealing and screaming at you. It's a good test to see how strong a Christian you really are. You see God gave me all His attributes to deal with every eventuality to stand and represent Jesus at work so that I could never let him down. In retailing you get a glimpse of society first hand. One time, we had our lives seriously threatened. The police had to surround our home and fitted special police alarms to our property. Some men came for me but the police were waiting for them. The men got away but they left the area, because the police were onto them. We get thieves messing themselves at the counter when caught, also shouting, fighting, running, in organized gangs and the like, too numerous to mention. Through all this kind of chaos, I kept my peace, because the end product is money and I had given it up and put it in better hands than mine – Jesus. We had security gates installed in the garden centre. An alarm sounds when people try to leave without paying for goods. For the first year we monitored it every time the alarm was activated. We were astonished when we caught one hundred and forty stealing in the first year. Some of the culprits were friends and regulars (regulars because they were stealing every week). We were shocked at the status of some of these people who were stealing. There were rich and poor from all walks of life. Here's an example: a wealthy man set the alarms off, so I asked him, if he had something he had not paid for. He said, No. I insisted that he must have. I will never forget this very rich man shaking as he emptied his pockets. There it was an article worth only sixty nine pence. It didn't make sense, because he could afford to buy the whole garden centre. Why, did he try to steal? As a Christian I understood why: As he stood there at the shelf he picked up the item, the tempter the devil spoke into his mind suggesting that he put it in his pocket, it's only a small item, they will never know. So because he hadn't the power of God through Jesus Christ in his life he himself could not override the temptation. Common sense doesn't work in these situations even though he was wealthy; the solution is Jesus in your life, only He can override the temptation when it comes. The man believed the lie that he wouldn't be caught, but the devil lied and wanted him caught, shaking with embarrassment over such a cheap item. Then I, as a Christian, would kick the devil into touch by forgiving folk when they stole, because the devil hates forgiveness. I would tell them there is a better way to live through Jesus Christ.

I hope the reader understands this example of the spiritual battle that takes place in all of our lives day and night. To confirm no matter who you are or what your standing is in the world, we are all tempted to sin. God is no respecter of persons or positions He sees us all equally. So we all need Jesus to overcome the wiles of the devil, by no other way can you overcome the tempter and be redeemed back to God our Father.

Moving on

The first assembly I belong to I left amicably with prayers and thanksgiving. Then after a brief period I joined another. But it didn't last long, because the establishment of this assembly came against us for working on a Sunday. We carried on working as normal, and then they sent one of the leaders to see us on the Sunday while we were working. He said we should not be working this day and then he took me on one side and prayed for me on the subject of working on the Sabbath. Unfortunately we had to leave their assembly, but before I left I explained to him that if I worked any day for the wrong reason, I would be sinning, not just on the Sabbath. I went on to explain that my church was open seven days a week, glorifying God through His business and my life. Every day is the Sabbath in my life, because I have retired from my work to do His work and will, totally retired in the Lord, to set an example even when chaos is all around me. You see Jesus is not only with me every day, but every moment of the day, not just one day a week but every day of the week, for the rest of my life.

> In Hebrews 4:9–10 it says 'There remained therefore a rest to the people of God. For he that is entered into his rest, he also hath ceased from his own works, as God did from his'.

As God rested on the seventh day, I have also entered through my salvation into the seventh day of rest. God rested and so have I, retired in the Lord, working and doing everything unto him, not for or of this world, but for his glory I live. I am now consumed with so much joy and peace, that work is not recognized any more, you just can't see it. My reward is eternal life saved from this body of death, everything now that I earn is for His kingdom and glory. I am not a man-pleaser, but a God-pleaser.

> Colassians 2:16–17 says, 'Let no man therefore judge you in meat or in drink, or in respect of a holy day, or of the new moon, or of the Sabbath days. Which are a shadow of things to come; but the body is of Christ'.

> Colassians 2:20 says, 'Wherefore if you be dead with Christ from the rudiments of the world, why, as though living in the world, are you subject to ordinances'.

These scriptures speak for themselves. I am dead to this world and I now live in the kingdom of God, saved from this world, so it is impossible to live to ordinances of the world, because I am not of it. Neither should you judge because of it. If you do you are still of this world and don't understand the kingdom of God. I also pointed out that if a child was injured in an accident on the Sabbath, which is technically Saturday, would you not call an ambulance? Obviously, yes you would. So, Christians in this example, who still live in the old dispensation, would you accept people working on the Sabbath? Or would you let the child die on the road? Jesus said, 'You hypocrites'. Would you not also call the fire brigade if your house was on fire on the Sabbath? What about doctors, nurses, police, army and airlines? Burglars would have a field day on the Sabbath, with no lights, or police. So many people are working behind the scenes, on the things you take for granted, so are you saying these millions of people can work for your security and comfort, but they cannot be Christians if the Sabbath is not to be worked on.

The Lord then answered him, and said, 'Thou hypocrite, doth not each one of you on the Sabbath loose his ox or his ass from the stall, and lead him away to watering'? (Luke. 13–15)

So God knew of the things to come, so come on Christians get into the now, because there is even more to come. Stop hurting yourself by dwelling and kicking against the pricks of this world. Get into the safety of the kingdom.

The Wilderness Years

I left that assembly and I didn't attend another for nine years, because I was so disillusioned at the time with the churchy system, which, rightly or wrongly, I fought against. I was a fairly young Christian at the time, but I used to read my Bible and question why what I was reading wasn't happening in the church of God. The system troubled me so much, that it was like going along with a lie, I just couldn't stand it any more. I couldn't live the lie. The pulpit was being used to ridicule people personally, which is wrong. Although I wasn't having Christian fellowship I still lived the Christian life otherwise to the letter and reading my Bible every day. To be honest I even used to read the Bible whilst on the toilet!

We carried on working in the business, still running it God's way, but I must confess I wasn't the same, I was quieter and I wasn't witnessing as much. The years rolled by, the children had left home and my wife became ill. In fact because we thought it was serious I immediately put the garden centre up for sale, telling my wife that she was more important than the business. We went to see a doctor privately so we could get the results quickly. She was ill; but the results were not life-threatening. She later had treatment and an operation which was one hundred percent successful. We sold the business fairly quickly and retired into a new house at the age of fifty six, even before my wife's treatment. We couldn't believe the trans-formation to our lives that retirement brought, from working seven days a week to zero. I thought if God is in it, I'll not miss it. I could hardly believe that I didn't miss the business at all, from the first day of retirement. I had a lot of thinking time and I questioned and questioned God over and over again, saying come on God you haven't miraculously called me just to sit here. What are you preparing me for? What am I doing wrong? I got no answer for two years into my retirement and then it hit me, God had put me in the wilderness for nine years to learn two little words which meant so much.

I realized that I never really learnt my lesson from the beginning, the words were meekness and humility, I was humble in a lot of ways but not humble enough in all my ways, my hand went over my mouth again, I couldn't believe it, I'm shaking my head now as I write, it was like being in prison for nine years, but I knew I was guilty as charged. What a patient God. He wanted to reveal the power of His word to me, but I'd stood in judgment with a know-all attitude. In this state God couldn't reveal more of Himself to me, because it would have made my situation worse. I was like a horse in a stable with all the power and God wouldn't let me out, because I refused to wear the bridle. Without the bridle there was no control of the power or direction, which easily causes hurt and ill-feeling. God had kept me ticking over all those years waiting for the right time to put me back on track to carry out His purpose in my life, as I am doing now writing His word. On revealing this truth to me, everything came flooding back and I got an urgent desire to go back to fellowship with other Christians. It was strange, probably the wrong word, but we went out on Sunday evening in our new area to a local assembly but it was shut, we went to two more and they were shut too, so we went to my sister's to visit instead. Apparently I discovered that these assemblies only open on Sunday mornings, but in my heart I new there was an assembly out there that God would want me to attend. Then it hit me. I remembered the assembly where my elder brother had got married ten years earlier and after all those years I remembered that it was a pleasant service. So I went on my own and immediately I felt a warmth, I knew for sure that this was the Christian assembly that God wanted me to attend. The pastor came to speak with me after the service and I told him that I hadn't been to an assembly for a long time, I also mentioned my brother's wedding, which he remembered.

I went home and told my wife, so we attended the following week and she found it comfortable too, there are not many of us, but I have learnt so much from my pastor and I enjoy the assembly very much, although I am always on my guard about going back into my old ways. I would rather not attend if I did and I don't want to do that, because I have now got that sense of belonging back. Thank you Jesus. I still get people saying that I speak too much sometimes. My pastor knows and understands that it's just my enthusiasm for Jesus and my desire to speak the truth into every situation. It's not what I say that's wrong, it's who I say it to and when. My wife notices this and says, 'Don't you realize that they don't understand you? In fact I don't sometimes'. So the lesson is, words are wasted if no one hears or understands what you are saying, it's not the listener's fault; it's me without my bridle on, I must wait on the Lord. Thank you Lord for my refining in the wilderness.

My learning experiences

I beseech you therefore, brethren, by the mercies of God, that you present your bodies a living sacrifice, holy, acceptable unto God, which is your reasonable service. (Romans, 12:1)

Sacrifice means dying to self, and then no one can hurt you any more, or get a selfish response from you, because self doesn't exist. You see people are self-centreed, instead of God centred. The me, me, me, attitude has got to go, if you want to be like and to follow Jesus.

Customers used to say to me, 'It's OK for you. You are rich'. My reply was always the same, that Jesus had changed my values. So what is rich? As an example I would say, 'If a blind man offered you a billion pounds in exchange for your eyes, would you accept it? Without thought they always said, "No, of course not"'. I then used to say to them, 'So that means you have a billion already, plus you have your arms and legs. Children come to my centre in wheelchairs, laughing and happy. So go and have a conversation with them about what is rich, or go and visit the children's hospital'. You need Jesus in your life as I did, to change your values. Just be grateful that you are whole'. A saying I have is, 'You don't know or value what you've got till you've not got it'. So I used to conclude that they also needed Jesus to change their values also and to open their eyes and be grateful and thankful for small mercies. They always left the centre a lot happier.

People also say to me, 'It's OK for you. You are a success'. This word, success, is mentioned around the world, but my opinion is this. I believe in God that success is an illusion, a lie; I accept that people in their own mind and personal life can think that they are successful and keep it to themselves; I can go along with that. But I tell you the truth, from my experience, after thirty years in business with moderate wealth, from a working-class background and with no debt. Would you say that my circumstances would be classed as a success in life? Or have I attained the imaginary figure? Or am I a penny short. If you say to people, 'I am a success', they may say, 'Define success'. You then may say, because you have more money than them. They may then reply that you haven't got as much money as Bill Gates, so you are not a success. I could say perhaps not but we still feel we are a success. So outwardly is success, position, money, health, property, beauty, cars, jewelry, tattoos, piercing, hair, clothes, your house, where you shop, the way you speak, your intelligence, where you came from, where or what you eat. I believe it's a personal thing of how you feel and not a competition about money or with others. If it was a competition and only about money, only the richest man in the world would be classed as a success. If you manifest these things to people, living your so-called successful life, I'm greater than thou attitude, you live in the pride of life. Worldly success only attracts, envy, jealousy, hate, with no real friends and sometimes loneliness. What is the point having success, where cancer and death cancels it out? Or being successful and going to hell. I personally know that success is only found in my saviour, Jesus Christ and to have His indwelling and attributes, (heaven on earth). Only then can you set a humble example that others might admire, love and follow, these values are greater even than the whole amount of money, silver or gold of this world.

For what is a man profited, if he gain the whole world, and lose or forfeit his own self? (Luke 9:25)

There is no comparison to Jesus, who stopped time with His humility and death, overcoming death on the cross so that you may be with Him in Heaven one day, sinless, because He loved you first, just as you are. There is only one success that has any eternal value that is to be reconciled with Jesus one day in heaven. Alleluia.

Speaking God's word into people's lives

Many people came to see me with many problems. They used to say, 'I don't know why I've come,' but they came anyway. I would pray for them and on every occasion, Jesus would give them the perfect answer for their problem, even I was gob-smacked at the wise words that He gave me to speak into their lives.

God would speak to me in my sleep. I always told my wife what He had said, because she would then encourage me. On one occasion God told me to pray for a woman with skin cancer. That very same morning she was the first in the centre, I just walked up to her and asked, 'Do you believe Jesus Christ can heal you?' She said, 'Yes'. I then said, 'Be healed in the name of Jesus'. I then walked away. She came to see me a while later and said that she was in remission. Alleluia. On another occasion the same again happened. Jesus spoke to me, the man in question was there in front of my eyes as I walked into the centre. This man was a pastor from another church. With trepidation I asked to speak to him. Over a coffee I told him that Jesus had told me to tell him to throw away his wig. I expected him to be furious, but he calmly said, 'I appreciate your concern, but I lost my hair when I was nine years old, when I lost my father and it never grew back. So I've worn a wig ever since'. He knew all the scriptures on the matter, regarding, vanity and that God loves you just as you are, perfect in his sight and adhering to this world with shame at being bald. I told him that only Jesus loves him enough to tell him the truth and that Jesus had called me, his servant, to relay this truth to him, and to remind him that nobody in the whole world and in your life might ever have told you this truth, but Jesus. I also told him that people were laughing and ridiculing him behind his back, some people only saw his wig and didn't take him seriously when he was speaking, saying he says he is a Christian, but he is false. To my knowledge he is still wearing his wig. I ask, how can you get close to Jesus, or represent Him if you can't even throw your wig away, or anything representing vanity, you represent Jesus who gave much more, His life.

Again one morning as I jumped out of bed, I said to my wife, that God had told me that this certain couple were going through some difficulties. I went to the meeting on Sunday as usual but they weren't there. I immediately got up and went to their house, sat them down and I just told them everything that Jesus had told me. They were totally shocked that I knew of their problem to put it mildly. They said, 'Only the pastor knew of our problem. Has he told you'? I said, 'No, God, through Jesus Christ, told me'. I went on to say that when I was younger I had gone through a similar experience, so that I spoke with a lot of understanding and compassion of what they were going through. I went to see them several times more, when they had come to the realization that God had sent me his servant to help them in their trouble. I told them that God must absolutely love them so much, that he saw their predicament and sent me his servant to share His love and compassion and to mediate for Him. I was personally moved by their predicament, such love, oh such love God had for them. God wanted them together for His reason and plan and God wasn't going to allow the adversary to spoil it. I just sat between them one day, things weren't going well for them, and intervened in their conversation, pointing out that they were doing the devil's work for him. He wants us to do his dirty work by fighting each other and to take control of all our lives. What we don't realise we can blame each other, but it's the devil who created the circumstance that we are falling out over in the first place, so who are we blaming the instigator or ourselves. It's not easy sometimes when we are tested to such a degree; to resist temptation, there is only one place to go: that's the foot of the cross, because that's where the power of forgiveness is. It's not easy to forgive sometimes, particularly yourself, which I personally found very difficult. So receive forgiveness as Jesus forgave us from the cross and then each other. Whatever you do don't waste that sacrifice that He gave for you. I am pleased to tell you that they were redeemed back into the safe hands of Jesus and are going on in the Lord mightily and stronger from their experience, because Jesus found time just for them. Today I see this couple's life as ambassadors for Christ, I don't know if God has revealed the true picture of their circumstance at that time to them. You see it wasn't what I said, or did personally, but it was the realization of Jesus' miraculous intervention, knowledge, love and presence, relayed through me to them. In other words Jesus wanted them to know that He felt their pain and He had sent His comforter, the Holy Spirit, to intervene and restore on their behalf. God always turns these circumstances to good, that good is that He wants people to declare to the world, with their heads up high, not guilty, or ashamed, simply that Jesus was there for them, yea just for them, when they needed Him. Their faith was weak at the time, but they saw with their own eyes, and heard with their own ears, the miraculous work of Jesus divine intervention in their lives, because of *love*. I encourage others to share abroad that same love and comfort that they had received, With your witness, others who are hurting like only you know and understand, might themselves come to the realization that Jesus is there for them also and has the answer to all life's woes. Alleluia.

Note, they were there for us too encouraging us in our ministry over the years. For example, they wrote to us when we retired and while we were in the wilderness years of our lives, in October 2002. At the end of the letter they write, 'Norman and Brenda, at this period in your lives just be open to God's plan for your future. He wants to continually bless you and your family and as you start this new chapter don't be afraid of the uncertainties, because the God who you both love and serve will lead and direct you in His perfect plan for your lives. Remember these verses from Proverbs 3:5–6, that we have shared together down the years,

> Trust in the Lord with all your heart and lean not on your own understanding; In all your ways acknowledge Him, and He will make your paths straight.

With Love. Alleluia. Thank you Lord for them, again this letter was sent with perfect timing. Don't we just need each other.

One evening I was sat in the lounge with my wife and children watching the television, when out of the blue, Jesus spoke to me and said that this particular man is planning to commit suicide. Again I was gobsmacked. I immediately told my wife – I call her my encourager, because she reminds me that everything I have said has always come to pass. My argument was, 'We can't ring them at this time of night. They live miles away', But my wife said, 'What about the circumstances, if you don't ring?' So with trepidation I rang them. To my relief the man's wife answered and I told her that her husband was planning to commit suicide. Then I said, 'What are your plans?', and she said, 'I am coming to Yorkshire with the children tomorrow and I'm leaving my husband on his own'. So I then told her not to leave him on his own, but to insist he came too, or not to come at all. Again I said, 'Whatever you do don't leave him on his own', which she didn't, I found out later. I can't believe how calm she was when I rang her with this devastating news. She was so matter of fact about it, she just said, 'Ok I'll not leave him on his own'. About three months passed and this man, who I said was going to kill himself, came into my business and asked to see me privately. I took him into my home which was on site and in private and he said, 'How did you know that I was going to commit suicide'? I said, 'Were you'? And he said, 'Yes.' He then said, 'How could anyone in the entire world have known what I was planning'. I said, 'Someone not of this world called Jesus Christ spoke to me, telling me of the devil's plan and caused me to intervene in your very life, with a simple phone call, because you weren't listening at the time'. I said, 'Don't you realize how much Jesus loves you and your family, using me His obedient servant to change the course of history in you and your family's lives?'. He didn't say much. He just shook my hand and then left, but I've seen him on and off over the years, bless him. As I write this even now I start to realise how profound God's intervention was in their lives, with that one phone call on the very night before the planned suicide. It was God's perfect timing, thank you Jesus for them.

I have written to them recently because, I still think, well I know that they have not grasped what happened and the consequences if God hadn't intervened. I am still convinced that God must have an enormous plan for their lives, but yet not revealed it to them, can you imagine the miraculous testimony of God's intervention in their lives? They could help others in the same predicament. Hold this space, because we have just been invited to their daughter's wedding. Just a thought, if God hadn't intervened he wouldn't be walking his daughter down the aisle. Alleluia. Before they left Yorkshire, they came to see me to say goodbye, I took them on one side and told them, 'If it doesn't work out don't blame yourself, and don't forget what I have said'. You can see with that statement God knew the future and that it wasn't going to work out, but it also told me that God through Jesus Christ was and still is with them today and for ever. And to think people say there is no

God. I know different, so does my wife and children who were present and witnesses to the miracles.

On another occasion, a man in dire need was introduced to me. I just loved him instantly. Through Jesus I paid off all his debts, and got all his services switched back on to his flat. God gave him a chance and put him in a position where he could glorify God for what He had done for him, with no more worries or fears any more. This man had been in prison for robbery and serious assault. He insisted on paying me back by doing occasional work in the garden centre. Because he insisted, I agreed. I thought I was very wise about giving, but I learned a lot from this man, because without thought, whatever he wanted, I gave him. My wife began to get pretty concerned about this. He carried on helping in the centre while we were away on holiday. But when we came back we realised that we had been robbed. My wife said it was this man that we had helped. But I would not have any of it and I carried on helping him to get back with his wife and coming to the Christian assembly. Shortly after, on the way back from church, God confirmed in my mind it was him, just as my suffering wife had said. Alleluia, the penny dropped. So the next morning, when he came to work, I confronted him and told him I knew it was him who had stolen from us. I just put my arms around him and told him that I still loved him, but not what was in him and that I could still help him. He then walked away and shouted, 'Never, never', in a loud voice. The next thing the police phoned me, saying this man was in hospital, he had tried to commit suicide, because of guilt, but he only gave the police my number. I phoned my pastor and he advised me not to go. The pastor said that I had done enough and that he would go instead. I never saw the man again, but I did hear of him. A pastor from another church came to see me and enquired of him in my life. Then he revealed he had attended their church collecting money and he had robbed them also. You can help

people but you can't live their lives for them. The moral of the
story for me, is that I still loved him, no matter what, and I
still do, only because I have Jesus in my life. In my old life I
wouldn't have given anything to him and I certainly would
have had him locked up. Could you in these circumstances, still
love and forgive him? Well I will tell you the truth: who am I
not to love and forgive him? Jesus forgave my sins no matter
what, and still loves me no matter what. Alleluia. When you
give, the responsibility is with the giver, you must carefully
assess each person you help and in what capacity, quietly,
openly, a kind word, encouragement, financial etc. In some circumstances it is better just to be on the sidelines, because some
people have to suffer before they can learn. Some people feel
they want to repay you, and some people can't. You have to
very careful, or you could lose some dear friends, although you
have helped them. You personally could get very hurt, so make
sure you help for the right reason, your reward is in heaven, for
God's glory we live. Alleluia.

One time a lady in our assembly (not my present assembly)
said, 'I have to tell you, because of respect, that my husband is
stealing off you every week at night time'. I immediately told
her to tell him that he is forgiven, she said, 'What He is forgiven
just like that?', I replied, 'Yes. Go quickly and tell him that he is
forgiven when you go home'. A few weeks later this man was
there as I opened my eyes in a prayer meeting, he just said, 'I'm
the man who has been stealing from you'. He went on to
explain, that after the security men had left, he used to steal my
goods. I immediately shook his hand, and said that God had
forgiven him though Jesus Christ, I told him to just accept that
forgiveness and to stop stealing'. He came down to my business the very next day, and said, 'I have not met anyone like
you'. I replied, 'Not only has God forgiven you, he now wants
me to give you a bible'. He went on to say, 'I have been robbing
you and instead of wanting recompense, you are giving some-

thing to me; it doesn't make sense'. I explained to him, that God is not of this world's system and that he actually stole from God himself and that it was Jesus in me that forgave him, not actually me, but Jesus in me. He said, 'How can that be that I have stolen from God'? I explained, that when I was saved I gave up everything, even the garden centre, where he was stealing, so it doesn't hurt me any more, because it's not mine, it's now in better hands than mine. It is not that I gave up everything, but it's a realization that it wasn't mine in the first place, because we own nothing, not even our selves, because we are temporary. This man stopped stealing and said he had never been better off since he stopped, he started to attend a Christian assembly and became a very close friend, and he would do anything for me. Thank you Jesus for him.

Marriage

This is my personal view of marriage after thirty seven years with my beautiful wife, friend and colleague. My wife Brenda had to have some of the virtues of patience and tolerance, when we met, or we would not be together today. I know she must and still does love me to have put up with me all these years. She is such a humble person, naturally quiet and one who very rarely raises her voice. She has always been a caring person naturally, but on the other hand, she is very easily hurt, although today she is much stronger in that department. She has brought up my two daughters, who she dotes on and helps them, even today. She is always there for them no matter what, she rings them every day. What hard work and sacrifice she has made for them, all because of love. Many people have let her down: her family and me, after we were only married a couple of years, I committed adultery and left her for a short time; but she eventually took me back. It was probably the best thing that happened to me, because I came to my senses, realizing how much I loved her. All these years have past, and she has never, I mean never, brought the past up and used my infidelity as a weapon against me. What a woman and I nearly lost her. Anyway working together for over thirty years, we rarely had any disagreements and if we did it was usually over business matters and not personal. We fell out more when I became a Christian as I explained earlier, but today we have such peace and contentment in our early retirement from work, giving us more time for others, looking forward not back, fixing our eyes on

Jesus. There are exciting times afoot for my girls, because Davina is getting married this year and Vanessa next year and then maybe there will be some tiny little feet!

In Genesis 2:24 it says 'Therefore shall a man leave his father and his mother, and shall cleave unto his wife, and they shall be one flesh'.

I've heard people preach on the sexual viewpoint of one flesh, but that's only part of it. Couples get confused by thinking sex is love. Sex should be an extension of love for each other. A lot of people get married for sex which is a physical thing that you have to keep doing to keep your marriage alive, which is impossible. That is why the divorce rate is soaring. Only love can keep you together in the difficult times that we all have in life. Don't fight it because that's how life is. Just thank God that there is a power called love, which overcomes and keeps us together no matter what, even to and beyond the grave. I see one flesh as being together in all things, you must be totally unselfish in marriage, so you must think of your spouse from the moment you wake up, every morning and all of your life and not your selfish self. You have got to want to please each other, not look for what the other can do for you. That attitude (get me . . . fetch me . . .) leads to an unbalanced marriage. God's way is that you want to please each other all the time, so you are looking for things to please your partner, without looking for reward. Your spouse recognizes this and then wants to naturally please you; by considering you all the time. You notice this, which stimulates you in wanting to please her. It goes on and on desiring to please each other, receiving love, consideration and understanding in all things from both partners, so you are constantly receiving from each other, but eventually it should become a natural way of life. So your thoughts are totally on and for your partner all the time and so becoming one flesh as God intended – a marriage, we say, made in heaven. Alleluia.

Representatives visited my business and their happiness was based on whether they had sold anything or not, so they were up and down likes yo-yos, depending on the value of their sales. I used to tell them that for years I too used to live this life, pushing for more of this world, not knowing why I was working and pushing so hard. I became oblivious to why or what I was doing, even life itself. I never stopped to have a good look at myself and take stock of my very life, because I was lost and blinded in the world's systems so called life. I know of many rich people who are still pushing for money they don't need. They are lost in this world. There are also people living beyond their means, trying to be something artificially, trying to make themselves look bigger than they really are in a worldly sense. That they are not; these people live the lie, spending more money than they earn. The lie I mentioned is that these people think that living this life will never catch up with them and they will never be found out. Usually these people hurt those people closest to them, but are oblivious to their hurt and suffering. I personally used to get seriously obsessed with the weather forecast and seasons, because the weather affected my sales and so my happiness was partly dependent on the weather. How futile can you get? I was locked into the world's system of I want, I've got to have. It's strange it's but the goal you have set yourself in life: that car, or that house, telling yourself that when you get them you will then be happy. I tell you now that that's a lie, because when you get them you still won't be satisfied. You will just take them for granted and want more, still pushing yourself into an early grave. I know by personal experience that nothing of this world can satisfy your soul. There is nothing wrong with material things, it's only wrong when you make these things your life and happiness as I used to do. I believe if you work hard you deserve the rewards of your labour. I tell my children that it is a criminal offence to waste your hard-earned money. In the truth of creation, if you put Jesus in your life, everything you have is more appreciated and not taken for granted, even your-self. Not only that, you stop pushing and wanting of this world, you become more content and satisfied, with that which only Jesus can give. I write like this because I know the difference. Every day in your life can become a good day, with no strife and pressure, because you can smile within you and say, 'Thank you Jesus for your peace', even if there is chaos all around you. You can stop dwelling on and looking at other people's lives, at what they have, and you can start to fully appreciate positively what you have instead, maybe your husband or wife, your children and grandchildren. You are warm, with a roof over your head and food on the table, your marriage will blossom in this con-tentment. Ask yourself, what happiness is, what constitutes it. Is it all the stuff you have acquired, that you have to keep buying to give you temporary happiness? Or is it that collection of thimbles, toys, pigs, teapots, that you spend your life search-ing for? Or do you want to be a star? What, you are not satis-fied? Go on then be a superstar. Still not satisfied? What about a megastar then? What, still not satisfied? This is your last chance of temporary worldly happiness, you are stretching it a bit, but go on . . . What about being a legend – yes I would love to be a legend – Sorry that is out of bounds and not attainable in this life, because when you are a legend you are dead. So you will not know of it, and I'm sorry to say that you won't be able to glory in it. So you'll never be happy then. True, there is no happiness in this world whatever position you are in, I tell you it's meaningless without Jesus controlling your life. I tell you the truth and I know that it's an inner joy of contentment and happiness of thankfulness and peace within you, with no pur-chase having to be made, because Jesus paid the price with His own life on the cross, you don't have to purchase anything any more to be happy, because the price of happiness has been paid in full, on the cross. You may start to smile again within you, just on your own, without a goody bag, it's hard for me, reader, because I'm trying to put into words of how I feel, and my desire is for you to feel the same. So give your life to Jesus and then you will know, it will cost you nothing, because only He can satisfy your heart's desire and then I will rejoice with you. Thank you Lord Jesus.

Anyway getting back to the salesmen I used to say to them, I bet you go home when you have not sold much, throw your briefcase in the corner and slump in the chair in a mood. Your poor wife, who's done nothing wrong, then takes the brunt of your so-called bad day, so your wife in these circumstances is in great trepidation, waiting for you to come home. In this situation you are allowing the circumstances of your job to control your happiness, plus your relationship with your wife and family. They usually laugh at me, because it's exactly what most of them did so. I wonder if this situation also applies to you, because this situation can double up if both partners are working and coming home with the same attitude, bringing the problems of work home: your relationship suffers, in your self-ishness. So when you go home from work be honest and say to your partner, I've had a bad day, or a good day, but thank God that I have you to come home to. Give your partner a hug. It will make such a wonderful difference to your relationship. So don't allow the pressure of your job to put a wedge between you. Even worse, what if you have had a bad day at work and the football team you support have also lost and you have been shouting obscenities at the opposition's fans; the police have had to keep you apart with dogs and horses and the like to stop you fighting . . . Are you listening you so-called supporters? *It's only a game*! Are you nuts? Are you sure you are human?

Oh to be born at fifty with more sense, because you have got rid of a lot of the dross from your life – such peace. Yes, age is a good remedy and learning curve, but again all you need is Jesus, because He has all the answers to life's circumstances and ills. I tell you the truth, give your life over to Jesus and He will put your life in order, as He did mine. Don't put your job or your local team before your wife or husband, don't live a futile life and live to statistics. Love each other in all circumstances. Keep close and treasure each other. If something goes wrong, and it will, that's life; look back to your wedding day where you were tied together in love, analyze what is going wrong, both speak the truth. I emphasize the truth only in the situation, because of love for your partner. Be prepared to make changes even sacrifices, for each other. Put your troubles in the bin where they belong. Fight the good fight for your marriage. Don't be a failure. Don't be a statistic. Walk into the sunset together. They say that a leopard can't change its spots, and that's true, the leopard can't. But we are not leopards! I got things wrong when I was young, as we all do sometimes. I changed my life and now we are in the sunset years. So let me encourage you, I did it, so you can do it also.

Parents

It fascinates me when I observe the changes that have taken place in my lifetime. Poor places around the world have still not got the standard of life, that I had sixty years ago. For instance, we had gas lights, I got washed in a pot dish with a fire under it, and my mum did all the cooking on the coal fire and did all her washing by hand. There were no telephones or televisions in our area at the time, no shampoo, nor toothpaste; there was no central heating or double glazing. Ice used to form on the inside of the glass in my bedroom. They used to sell from horse and carts in the street, and we used to help my mum make rugs out of old rags. My father was a Welshman and moved to Yorkshire, where he met my mother, to work in the mines. He worked very hard to give us a reasonable standard of living. When he died, I realized after looking through his papers that he had been in the army twenty years exactly, reaching a position of Provo Sergeant and he was mentioned in dispatches for bravery. I was born just after the second world war finished, in December 1945.

The reason that I'm writing this is that these circumstances in my life and my relationship with my father might help someone else in similar circumstances. I hardly had a conversation, or love from my father. My relationship with him was zero. But at the time, when I was young I thought it was normal. He was very strict with us; we daren't speak at the table when eating, and we certainly had to eat everything that was put in front of us, or else. He was always in transit, either going to work, to bed or to the pub. He wasn't a big drinker and I never once heard him swear; he never sat down with us as a family, apart from eating. I discovered that I was given my middle name, Norman, after his beloved corporal in the army, who was killed on the front line at my father's side. He told me the story (he didn't tell many) that they thought he was only wounded, so they carried him back off the lines to medical tents, where they laid him down with the rest. He said you wouldn't want to see or hear the noises made in that medical camp. It was frantic. My father then went out side for a smoke while they tended to his friend and soon after, as he looked up outside at the other end of the tent, he saw the medics throwing his beloved corporal on to a wagon with the rest of the dead. He ran up and dragged him off the wagon into his arms, and said, 'What are you doing? Get off him.' They replied, 'I'm sorry Sarg. But he is dead'. 'He can't be', my father said. They just said, 'Sorry Sarg'.

My father had died before I could understand him as a Christian does, but now I can understand him. Can you imagine what he had suffered and seen? You probably can't; neither can I. Whenever he looked at me as a teenager, he compared me to his corporal. No wonder he had so much contempt for me. How could I compare to him. He never ever said one kind word to me, and I know now that within himself he had died in the war, he had seen and done too much, with horrific memories. What helped me was an old man on the television talking about his life in the first world war. He was only seventeen at the time and was on burial duty. He said that as the men went forward on the lines, a lot were killed and wounded, but you couldn't get to them, because you would be killed too. Their cries for their mums and for God, which tapered off in the night, as they slowly died still echoed in his ears. When he and other eventually got to some of them, sometimes after months, rats used to jump out of the cavity of their chests. This man on the television was originally asked why he didn't marry, to which he replied. 'I died in the war. Too many memories. I saw and heard too much. I died with them I buried, such sorrow I was no good to no one, my memories keep me in a quiet death'. You just can't go on and live a normal life after being in the horrors of war. The programme finished and I said to myself, 'That was my dad'. He too died in his war.

The programme gave me great understanding and compassion for my father, setting me free to forgive and love him. I just want to put my arms round my father, something I never did in my entire life, and tell him that I understand. But it was too late. He had gone, I missed my father's love, I know there is no point me crying now, but I can't help it, writing it has made it more real to me. Thank you Lord for filling the void. I hope this real life story will help other people to understand that everyone loses something in war, particularly my beloved mother, who was on her own many years during the war.

My wife's parents lived locally and helped in the café in our centre, until they got too old to manage. Being a Christian broke a lot of barriers down, enabling me to love them and kiss them. My father-in-law had never flown, so I took him on a day trip to Rome, in his seventies, which he enjoyed very much, he wrote to us to thank us for the trip, 'To Brenda and Norman. Thank you both so very much for one of the most memorable days of my life. Unforgettable. I still can't believe I have been to Rome and back in one day. Once again I thank you both so very much a thousand times. I love you and God bless you. Your loving Dad. PS: That hug and kiss at home meant a very lot, Norm, at the end of the day.xxxxxx'. That's Jesus. Thank God for them both.

Kids and society

We were so happy playing in the street with the other kids, it was that good we never wanted to go to bed. It was all we knew and it cost nothing. We never had to lock our doors. People used to talk more; to be honest there wasn't much else to do. There was a baby born next door at the same time as my sister was born and because his mother couldn't breast feed him, my mother breast fed them both. Can you imagine that happening today? It was 'the good old days' in some respect, there wasn't any I want, I want, attitude because there was nothing to want. Children today always seem to want something, fashion, or the latest gadget, to make them happy but they soon get bored with it. They are more disobedient, because there is less discipline. Love and discipline go together; one without the other doesn't work. We had a lot more peace and contentment, its how society has changed. I'm not surprised at man's ingenuity and intelligence because God made man in his image and put everything here in the first place, for man to discover. It's obvious, but God wouldn't have put anything here in the beginning, if he didn't want man to discover it, computers, telecommunications and the like. So here's a good question: Is life getting better, less stressful, easier, happier, more tolerant? Are we helping each other more? Is it safer on the streets for our kids? Every person can answer these questions themselves, depending on their personal opinion and status in life. For me I think in reflection, and as a Christian, we have more and still want more, which mankind thinks will make society and life

163

better, but in reality it's a lie, you cannot buy and have more on the outside, to give you peace and tranquility. It's the inside of man that needs to change. Why have inmates in the women's prisons doubled in the last twelve years? Is it because society is getting better? What's gone wrong? The government sits snugly in their righteousness, while people are hurting out there, promoting chaos and drunkenness on our streets and drugs in our schools. The government is trying to stagger the opening times of pubs and clubs as a remedy to stop everyone coming out of the pubs at the same time, so the police can cope with the fighting and drunkenness. They are now planning to stop us chastising our children in our own homes. Are they nuts? The next generation will be taking parents to court! Oh, what hope have the children without discipline? Who are these people? Do they know what they are doing? I don't think so. We have made the kids paranoid, they now think all adults are potential paedophiles, because we are not allowed to touch them. The devil is loving it, causing pandemonium throughout society, the world's gone mad. It's true that in our country we are getting more material wealth, but at what expense? Pressure, pressure, pressure. We have got to have, now which has created an uncaring, zombie society. The government scare-monger and tell us that they can't afford our pensions, in other words the money we have paid in has probably gone on overseas interference. In the next breath they take tax off gambling, encouraging people to gamble. Who are these people? You can't come out of our assembly without getting insults from the kids. They have just smashed the new windows. You have to ignore them, because if you don't it gets worse. The kids used to be frightened of punishment for what they did, but now they know society can't touch them, so they control the streets. They do what they want, when they want and get away with it. Forty percent of hospital staff have been attacked or abused, firemen and ambulancemen are attacked in the street and these are the caring people who are trying to help us. So what hope is there for the rest of us? The government has to keep changing laws and bring out new ones because of new crime and disobedience on our streets, but it's the government who has created this undisciplined violent society by their decisions. Kids don't do much exercise these days. They eat the wrong food, even in schools, and get overweight. It takes a caring restaurant owner to point this out to the government, before they do anything and change the diet in schools. Can you see what I'm trying to say, reader? Society itself creates new problems. By its own wrong decisions and ignorance. Then we have to try to come up with a remedy. What hope has the next generation got? Society has gone education mad, but with no discipline, pressurizing the kids to such a degree that they are robbing them of joy in their youth. Education is right, but the balance is all wrong. It's out of gear. It's got too serious. The kids have no time for leisure and themselves. I tell you there is more to life than just education. If education is the answer to society's problems, why is there more disobedience in our streets? Why can't joy be brought into learning? To some kids it's like a prison sentence and they rebel. So, I tell you the truth, as society degenerates, and there is no doubt it is doing so, there will be nowhere else to turn but to the rules and laws of God and His virtues, through the teaching and example set by Jesus Christ Himself, that has never changed from the beginning of time. So man, where is your excuse for changing and getting society all wrong with no discipline creating pressure and greed in our next generation? The only remedy is Jesus, who never changers.

The past

If only . . . Regrets, we have all had them. We have to get it wrong, to get it right, It's the only way to learn sometimes.

Although I was saved, the past still troubled me. You can sin and hide in it. Without exposure you can feel all right, because nobody knows. Many people are like this all their lives, even Christians who can't understand why they are not moving on in God. God knows of your secret sin which separates you from Him. God hates sin. So pray to God that your sin will be exposed. Exposure brings guilt, which should lead you to repentance and forgiveness, if you love God. Guilt can sometimes be a good thing, because it hurts and troubles you. If you are a caring person for yourself and others, your desire would be to want to eradicate guilt from your life. But Satan uses guilt as a weapon of past sin reminding you of it over and over again. So if you concentrate on the past of unforgiveness and guilt and let it trouble you, that past becomes present in your life, so you live in the past now, allowing those memories to trouble you now, affecting your mood, wishing and hoping for things you cannot change. The thing that set me free from the past as a Christian, was realizing that it is a spiritual life and the instigator of the pain of the past is the tempter – the devil, or evil spirits. He loves to remind you of past hurts and your sin, particularly in your quiet times. So who am I fighting for my sanity and normality? You don't have to fight. Just accept God's forgiveness, and forgive others. You can only do it through salvation, because it is impossible to forgive without Jesus in your life. Let me encourage you from Scripture

Fight the good fight of faith, lay hold on eternal life, whereunto thou art also called, and hast professed a good profession before many witnesses. (1 Timothy 6:12)

Be sober, be vigilant; because your adversary the devil, as a roaring lion, walketh about, seeking whom he may devour. (1 Peter 5:8)

For we wrestle not against flesh and blood, but against principalities, against powers, against the rulers of darkness of this world, against spiritual wickedness in high places. (Ephesians 6:12)

Jesus said, 'The thief cometh not, but for to steal, and to kill, and to destroy: I am come that they might have life, and that they might have it more abundantly'. (John 10:10)

So stop blaming yourself and others, it does no good. Shout, 'Not guilty', as I did, and start to live an abundant, good and fruitful life that you deserve, You know it makes sense. Alleluia.

To bring you up to date, this is not a fictional life that I write about, it's Jesus in my life. I couldn't write it if I personally didn't live and believe the words that I write. I accept people will come against this book, as they have come against me, but that's exactly what they did to Jesus and the prophets, so it's no different today. Sometimes I feel so lonely. God has shown me that as I walk down Calvary Road (where Jesus was sacrificed). He is saying, hold even tighter to my hand, abide in me closely as you walk further down my sacrificial road, and do not fear, because I've been there before you. I know that I have walked a long way, or God could not give me the inspiration to write to you.

As I represent Jesus more in my life, as Jesus did, I'm finding more verbal rejection, people seem not to understand me any more, even though I'm in God's will, doing good without reward, they see me, instead of Jesus in me. Yet I feel in good company, because Jesus was rejected, but still He sacrificed His life for all mankind, but He doesn't expect that of me. He says, just die to self and allow me to come in and take control of your life fully. Because of God I know I am loved no matter what my story is. My story is not your story; we all have to walk the same heavenly road, but we are all different, with our own story, but one in Christ. Yes, down this sacrificial road gets lonelier, because people are failing God in their sin and religion. Many are called, but few are chosen. So come on Christians, get walking. The kingdom needs you. If a man came into your midst and did good, and loved you unconditionally, served you, told you the truth and was on call twenty four hours a day, that man was Jesus Christ. But they still crucify Him over and over again. In my experience it is still happening today. Sorry reader if my testimony has taken so long, with some preaching, it's only because I care. I wanted to share with you some of the difficulties, trials and tribulations that I have been through in my life. I feel maybe it could help you, or bring people to know the Lord. Thank you.

Summary

To sum up without explanation of to what I have written, I will leave it for you to decide, that is your free will, I have written this book in tears and weakness, in obedience to God's command.

God wants to reveal Himself more to mankind at this time and maybe these simple truths of life that I have written will give you God's food for thought, regarding your personal life and our world. Maybe a new seed – namely Jesus Christ, I make no apology – will grow within you, creating a new beginning, a new person, as it did for me. You may think that you are insignificant in this world, and that you can't make a difference, but I tell you the truth, you can – but only through Christ can your purpose and potential be realized. I pray that all God's virtues through Jesus Christ will be overflowing in your life and that others might see the difference in you.

May God be with you, guard you, bless you all the days of your life. The kingdom needs you, remember it's your reasonable service.

Amen.